By The Tree

By The Tree

The Second Anthology of the Fayette Writers Guild

Published by HD-IMAGE

First published in North America by HD-IMAGE, 2005

PUBLISHER'S NOTE
These selections are works of fiction. Names, characters, places, and incidents are the products of the authors' imagination or are used fictitiously, and any resemblance to actual persons, living or dead, events, or locales is entirely coincidental.

ISBN 0-9770437-0-3

ACKNOWLEDGEMENTS

The Fayette Writers Guild presents its second annual collection of their works representing fiction, nonfiction and poetry in their individual and creative style.

Again the community of Fayetteville has been there to help and we wish to thank them for their contributions. They were Fayette Arts Center and Gallery, Kroger's, Barnes & Noble, and the Fayette Citizen.

It takes a great deal of dedication and energy from the members to make this writing group a success and we want to thank them for their many contributions as well. Hopefully 2006 will be just as much fun.

Carol Buckler, Founder & President
Blanche Babcock, Vice President
Carol Lunsford, Public Relations

CONTENTS

If you break the law, you end up in jail. I spent the first 8 ½ years of my life in jail! However, home was on the first floor, and the Jail cells were on the second floor!

At the time this did not seem unusual to me, but looking back on my life, I realize it was different and exciting. This is one reason I write. My children should know about their family.

My Daddy was the deputy sheriff in Sonora, a small town in the ranching country of West Texas. Facts and stories of our family need to be written down to be enjoyed and at the same time teach us how the past shapes our lives. These interesting and wonderful stories are a treasure to be saved for each generation. Family history is important!

Our values are learned early in life. I have vivid memories of prisoners being hauled off in the prison paddy wagon. This is something I'll never forget! When I tell my stories of my early life, my children will have a sense of who I am as I write about the funny or amusing things that happened along the way, and also about some of life's problems as I understood them.

I have a burning desire to write about the lives of the early Taylors, Wrights, Regeons and Babcocks, beginning with our ancestors and continuing on with present-day activities of my family, such as hunting in those West Texas hills, car racing, white water rafting on the Chattooga River in the Blue Mountains of North Georgia, and on and on.. .

I am presently continuing the research and writing of my family history. This is the follow-up to the large two-volume family book I produced in the year 2002.

It Really Was There On the Old Iron Bridge

As we drove up to within thirty-five feet of the bridge, Jack softly, but excitedly exclaimed, "Look, straight ahead on the old iron bridge!"

Sherry and I peered around Ken and Jack sitting in the front seat.

"Oh my gosh! A mountain lion! Just standing there," I blurted out with utter amazement. "I can't believe this! He's crouching there on the edge of the bridge, just looking at us. Wow, he's big!"

Did my eyes deceive me? Was he real?

I never imagined when Sherry and Jack suggested, "Let's go eat shrimp," at this restaurant, whose specialty is fresh shrimp, that the events which followed would be such a surprising outing for Ken and me on that hot sunny day in May!

Ken and I were visiting Sherry, our daughter and her husband, Jack, who lived in the small West Texas town of McCamey. It is located in the northeastern section of the Chihuahuan Desert, which extends down into Old Mexico.

"Sounds good!" I said, as we all climbed into the car. But to my surprise, I found out the seafood restaurant was located in Imperial, Texas, a forty-mile drive one-way further west into the desert. The shrimp farm, by the restaurant, is fed by an irrigation system from The Imperial Reservoir. The reservoir receives its water from the Pecos River. The reservoir and the water channels were constructed back in the early 1900's to help with the irrigation of the farms.

On the way to Imperial, we drove through drifting sand dunes, and we were on our way to eat fresh shrimp in the desert? It was the last place to look or expect to find shrimp.

At one time there were many farms in the area. They say the changing water conditions were part of the decline of the farms. I wonder? I had an eerie feeling, like something was lurking around the corner.

When we finished eating, Jack said, "How about we drive over and look at the 'Old Iron Bridge?'"

Ken, Jack, and Sherry had seen this part of the Pecos River many times. There is a lot of history where the Old Iron Bridge crosses the river.

Now on with the story where we meet up with this eye popping sight, a mountain lion on the Old Iron Bridge!

"Get your camera," Jack was saying at the same time I was fumbling with the zipper on my purse.

"Is he still there?" I whispered as I hurriedly grabbed my camera at the same time trying to turn it on.

"Yes, hurry up! He's still there!" Jack anxiously answered.

"Oh darn, what's wrong with this thing?" I muttered.

"Here, give it to me," Sherry said as I shoved the camera into her shaking hands. "The memory card is full!" she exclaimed.

I had used up the entire memory card earlier in the day, taking pictures of oil wells, jackrabbits, windmills, quail, and cactus flowers out on the ranch, but I distinctly remembered deleting the pictures from the camera after I had loaded them onto the computer.

What happened?

A strange feeling came over me! How could the pictures still be there? While the frustrating thoughts were bouncing around in my head, Jack reached back for the camera.

"The big cat is still there. Maybe I can ease out of the car and get a shot." Very silently Jack put one foot on the ground with camera posed to shoot.

Well, that was it!

The huge cat had waited long enough for us humans to take his picture. He dropped out of sight, just disappeared!

One minute he was there; the next minute he was gone, like a ghost! My eyes blinked several times to clear my vision.

Did I really see him?

Of course I did!

The picture of the big cat was etched on my brain. Coming to my senses, I joined the others as we all piled out of the car and fanned out as we ran toward the Old Iron Bridge, hoping we might get a glimpse.

No such luck!

He was gone!

"I think I heard a soft padding noise along the bank," Sherry exclaimed. I hadn't heard a thing!

My eyes darted here and there, straining to find the cat. We were thinking he could have gone down the bank to the river, but Lady Luck had deserted us. He may have doubled back behind us into that thick low brush," Sherry whispered.

"Darn! I know I deleted the pictures off the camera before we left the house," but there they were, still in the camera. Shivers went down my spine! Strange things were happening!

I was so disappointed that I had missed the picture of a lifetime, a mountain lion in the rugged desert country of West Texas.

What a beautiful and unusual picture the mountain lion would have made, framed by the "Old Iron Bridge."

"I goofed by not being ready," I moaned over and over as we climbed back into the car. I knew I would not hear the last of this.

I finally deleted all the afternoon pictures from the camera; a little late I admit, but this time they were gone, and I was now ready to take pictures of the bridge and the river, - but sadly no mountain lion!

Continuing on with our sight seeing, we followed the river a short distance to another historical sight, Horsehead Crossing, a camping place once used by Comanche, Kiowa and other Indians. Anglo-Americans used the crossing as early as 1839. The name Horsehead Crossing came from the many horses that perished from drinking too much bad water, and then plunged to their deaths over the steep banks of the river.

The cattle of the trail drives also had a similar fate. When the herd neared the river, the cattle smelled the water, stampeded over the cliffs or bogged down in the treacherous quicksand and died at Horsehead Crossing.

Were their other causes of the deaths of so many animals? Was nature responsible or something else?

Reading the historical concrete sign about "Horse Head Crossing of the Pecos River," which was erected by the State of Texas back in 1936, only increased my curiosity.

Below is a picture of the sign:

Horse Head Crossing On the Pecos River

Here crossed the undated Comanche Trail from Llano Estacado to Mexico.

In 1850 John R. Bartlett while surveying the Mexican boundary found the crossing marked by skulls of horses, hence the name "Horse Head" the Southern Overland Mail, (Butterfield) route, St. Louis to San Francisco, 1858-1861, and the road west from Fort Concho crossed here.

The Goodnight-Loving Trail, established in 1866 and trod by tens of thousands of Texas Longhorns, came here and turned up the east bank of the Pecos for Fort Sumner and into Colorado.

Erected by the State of Texas 1936

Ken as a small boy had met Colonel Goodnight and read the book, Charles Goodnight Cowman and Plainsman, by J. Evetts Haley, which peeked his interest in the history of the trail rides in this part of the country. The trail drive of 1866 led by Colonel Goodnight and his cowboys blazed a new trail for Longhorn cattle.

The most severe part of the drive of all the Texas trails began when Colonel Goodnight left Ft. Concho, where present day San Angelo, Texas is located. San Angelo is also my birthplace and my youngest daughter's. My ancestors settled in this part of Texas back in the late 1800's.

Colonel Goodnight and his cowboys followed the old route of the Butterfield Stage of past years. Its ruts had cut a path that pointed to Horsehead Crossing. Horsehead Crossing is 12 miles west of Castle Gap, a canyon about one mile in length. Horsehead Crossing is the most noted ford along six hundred miles of the Pecos. The Pecos River, no more than a hundred feet wide in any spot, runs through a vast arid countryside.

Spanish explorer Felipe de Rabago y Teran crossed this part of the Pecos country in 1761. Some of the California bound American travelers passed through Castle Gap and Horsehead Crossing.

Standing on that spot, I was mesmerized as Ken, Jack, and Sherry shared the pioneers' stories of adventures and hardships in the rough and wild country all around us. What courage and endurance the early travelers had.

The end of the cattle drives and modern road construction decreased the importance of Horsehead Crossing by the twentieth century. There was no more use for the bridge. Times and conditions changed. The planks were taken up, and all that is left today are the iron beams.

But today I know a spirit or a ghost or "my mountain lion" is guarding this territory! People tried to change this country into something else, but they failed. The river, the land, and the wild life are back like before white man began to settle into this area.

Leaving the Old Iron Bridge, Jack had another surprise for us. He knew how to get to an old abandoned cemetery not too far from where we were. The sun was rapidly sinking, but enough sunlight "as left to explore the cemetery.

A short distance off the highway, down a dusty road, we found the cemetery, pulled up to a gate, and stopped.

There were a good many unmarked graves, with just a few marked stones. I stopped and read this one: "ASA CALLAWAY 1901 – 1919"

The thought struck me how young this person was when he died - 18 years old! Why had he died? All the marked graves were those of young people.

"What had happened?" I silently thought. Why did the relatives just up and leave? No one was left to take care of the small cemetery. Did something scare them off? It looked like they abruptly left. It leaves one with an unsettling thought to think they never returned!

Thinking back to the pioneer days I realized it could have been so many things - like rattlesnakes, gun fights, lack of food and water, Indians, wild life (mountain lions or other predatory animals), disease brought on by the hardships and accidents of an isolated life with no doctor near by, just to name a few reasons. It was probably their strong sense of survival that caused the pioneers to suddenly leave this desolate county without a backward glance!

Moving on I counted 30 graves, each with an iron cross as a marker. There was no way to identify who was buried in each grave. The weeds and brush covered the area. Two or three of the gravesites even had animal burrows.

As we left the neglected little cemetery, the growing shadows told us our daylight hours were numbered. We hurriedly retraced our steps back to the car as the day turned into deep shadows, and the hot sun slowly sank below the horizon of the vast expanse of the dry sandy waste.

The drive home to McCamey became more relaxing as the distance grew from the Pecos River Country. The stars are brighter out there with no city lights to spoil the view. We could see for miles and miles in the distance. Jack and Ken pointed out the lights of oil wells, gathering stations for the gas and oil wells, and a small community.

When we arrived at Jack and Sherry's home from our evening out in the Pecos River country, I felt tired, but refreshed. This vast and desolate country life style is quite a contrast to the life we live in the busy and crowded city of Fayetteville, Georgia.

The next day we drove to Wink, Texas, twenty miles from the New Mexico line, to visit our granddaughter and her family. Sure enough the tale of "The Old Iron Bridge" had taken a different slant. My mountain lion had turned into a Bobcat, according to Jack, Sherry, and Ken.

I couldn't believe my ears. "That was a mountain lion," I protested.

They didn't completely ignore me, but continued on with their "Bobcat" version of the story. Well, I let them have their fun, knowing I was right. I lamented over and over, "If I had just gotten the picture, I could prove you are just spinning a yarn." I knew it was useless discussing the point any further, because the three of them stuck to their story of a "Bobcat" instead of a "Mountain Lion!"

However, just as all the Indians, horses, longhorn cattle, young people buried in that forgotten graveyard, which had once inhabited the Pecos River country, so does "my mountain lion." There may not be a sign erected by the State of Texas, or an old iron cross marking the mountain lion's passing, but my story stands!

It was a mountain lion out in the West Texas desert where shrimp are grown on farms, and mystery abounds in the sand dunes. On the old iron bridge near the setting of the sun under the big West Texas sky, it really was there, and it was a mountain lion!

Writing is a form of communication, so what is more important in friendship than communication.

Only a hermit keeps to himself, but even he has a tendency to write for posterity. Communicating by talking, we sometimes blunder and can't be easily corrected.

When we write we have the opportunity to re-do any errors.

I wish to share my thoughts and my personal adventures, hoping they give pleasure in the reading. Also I like to read works about their lives.

By writing I can share my life with all my family. My father was interviewed at age 84. It was taped and then typed. I was amazed at what I learned of his life, and was thrilled to learn something of his life. I admire so much his integrity and ability. He had some exciting experiences he was now able to share with me. I felt I should do the same for all my loved ones, who really know very little of my life.

My decision to write my story became an obsession with me as I started writing a little each day for two years! The more I wrote the more I remembered. I finally finished it and began editing and changing much I'd written, so the reader understood it better. That took another six months! I hope my family can enjoy this book, and hopefully others will enjoy it also.

I admire those with the ability to write funny things. It takes a different ability, and we enjoy their sharing fun. I love funny things and really enjoy a sense of humor. It tickles my tummy! Life is such a serious thing for us. We need a break once in a while, reading a good book can be a relaxing thing for us.

The Famous Indian Scout Charles Goodnight

In December of 1924 the government sent Daddy to the Goodnight ranch in the Panhandle Region of the state of Texas to check for parasites on buffalos and Cattalos.

Cattalo was a tentative name Colonel Goodnight had for the cross breeding of cattle with Buffalo. The buffalo and Cattalos were put in pens and Daddy went to work examining these animals for parasites and insects.

Daddy took my sister Gertrude and I along. Gertrude was twelve and I was just barely six. How exciting this trip was for us both. Daddy took us with him by train as four hundred miles each way in a Model T Ford in 1924 would have been a mighty long trip.

I remember how Colonel Goodnight looked when we met him: whitish whiskers, stained brown in spots by tobacco juice. He was rather small in stature (he was then in his 90's). He had a huge thick buffalo robe on the floor, and what a rug it was! It must have been 4 inches thick. Soon I heard Colonel Goodnight tell his foreman, Cleo Hubbard, to "take the kids for a buggy ride."

What fun that was! We rode around the Canyon in a real buggy, pulled by a horse. We had impressive rock cliffs and spires to see along the broad valley of the Palo Duro canyon. Also seeing Buffalo roaming the fields was quite exciting. We noticed there were wash-outs in the road, which were evidence of a recent cloudburst.

I read that there is a museum honoring Colonel Goodnight, virtually on the rim of the canyon. It is either in or close to the town of Canyon, Texas. Colonel Goodnight was quite famous in the late 1800s as a scout and Texas Ranger. The Colonel had studied nature and became an expert at understanding the action of all life in the wild country of North Texas. He never needed a compass but always knew his direction. Knowing nature so well, he was completely at home in the Wild West, scouting for fresh water and camping grounds for the Army or Rangers. As an example, he could often locate water by watching the flight of birds in the evenings.

About the end of the Civil War he and Mr. Loving joined together a plan to move cattle to New Mexico and Colorado to sell. They established a cattle trail west from San Angelo, Texas across the Pecos River, then north into New Mexico. These trails became known as the Goodnight-Loving cattle trails. This turned out to be a success and with that success Colonel Goodnight later established a big cattle ranch in the Palo Duro Canyon of North Texas. He became an outstanding rancher and leader for the cattlemen of Texas. He was highly respected by all, including members of the State Senate and House in the Texas State Capitol, which he often visited on business.

My Daddy and the Colonel became good friends from that 1924 visit and corresponded by letter until the Colonel died about four years later.   Mrs. Goodnight had died about 1925.

I was personally familiar with the Goodnight Loving trail passing about 12 miles North of McCamey, my home for many years.   I was a pilot and flew my airplane along the trail from San Angelo, Texas, (Old Fort Concho) then west from Fort Concho through Centralia draw north of what is now Big Lake, then on west through Castle Gap, which is north of McCarney, Texas.   The trail continues on further west from Castle Gap to Horse Head Crossing, on the Pecos River.   The trail continued on west and then north, following the Pecos River into New Mexico, where I flew no further up the trail.   The trail branched toward Colorado.   This trail was successful as it avoided the Staked Plains of Northwest Texas, where there were untold numbers of unfriendly Indians and open prairie.   The Comanche and Apache Indians frequently raided the plains area of New Mexico before the year 1900, by coming down from their camps in the New Mexico mountains and crossing into the Great Plains of North Texas.   There were Indian trails converging at Horse Head Crossing on the Pecos, on raids going all the way into Mexico where the Indians stole horses and took Mexicans with them as slaves.

The Comanche Indians killed Mr. Loving on one of these raids, catching him and a cowboy scouting ahead of a trail herd.   This happened where the Pecos River now crosses the Texas-New Mexico line. Loving had an arrow in him and couldn't travel, so the cowboy escaped by floating or swimming down the river at night, and went to the trail herd for help.   He reached Colonel Goodnight and his crew, but too late to save Mr. Loving's life. There is now a town called Loving in New Mexico only a few miles East of where Mr. Loving was killed.

When Colonel Goodnight started his ranch, he only had to fence across the canyon in the South and in the North, within the steep sides of the canyon. This effectively kept the cliffs and steep canyon walls serving as fences on both sides. Some of the Buffalo herd that ranged wild within the Canyon was later given to the Park Service.

Colonel was happy ranching and seemed to have an insatiable appetite to know all about insects attacking cattle and buffalo. He correctly found that cattalos were not bothered by the insects that attacked cattle.

Too bad this idea was not followed through before his death. As far as I know, no one has completed a study on Colonel Goodnight's studies.

In school I wrote essays in German, exercises in organizing thoughts and playing with words, and I enjoyed it. Then I wrote letters, before telephone time, reporting of places and people spiced with my viewpoint and my family encouraged with "interesting letters". Over time my audience and the experiences I drew on changed their worlds. It took me a while to be pleased with anything I wrote in English.

Writing is a humbling experience because of the awareness that words and thoughts arise from somewhere unknown, head for uncharted territory where the writer is in for the ride. That's how my poems, prose and stories come about; I consider them gifts.

Often my writing is stimulated by something I observe and I have learned to be vigilant for such incidences. Like the one on mother's day when I watched how a mother bird persuaded her child to flutter to safety. Wrapping pain in ambiguous poetry is a way to release pain and anguish. Light decorations, even a rainbow found their way into my yearly Christmas poem.

My writing is observing outside, and then looking inside for understanding of what I see and feel. Why I write? I need to share, to entertain. What my mind brings forth might have meaning to someone, stimulate new thoughts. Writing is for me like looking for a kindred spirit to grow with. Intent on giving words to what life brings forth, it is also my escape.

The Bird Cage

The train was quite empty. Walking the narrow passage I found an empty compartment. I closed the sliding door, and choosing the window seat looking back, I intended to enjoy the rhythmic sound and motion of trains.

I always wondered which direction was better, the one looking ahead, or the fuller view looking back. At the next station a man entered and took his seat opposite to mine.

Beside him, he set down an extraordinary birdhouse. Shaped like a three tiered oriental pagoda it was made of light colored wooden bars curved inward and outward that came together on the top like the golden dome of a cathedral. An exquisitely carved door had golden hinges and a golden knob and its floor had flowers and green branches painted on it, as if it were a meadow. Two tiny bowls seemed anchored to the side, opposite the door, as if for food and water. I was curious what precious bird would reside in that palace.

The tall, slim man might be 50 years old, his hair slightly thinning and graying at the temples. Behind modern small glasses were brown eyes. He wore a tweed jacket, striped gray shirt, beige pants and brown European leather walking shoes. The conductor came to check our tickets and after that, the man did not take to huddling in his window seat and did not close his eyes.

What bird will live in this beautiful bird house? I ventured, wanting to entertain myself conversing with a fellow traveler.

The man's answer surprised me.

No bird ever lived in it and will not now. Birds should be free, not imprisoned in a cage inside a house.

"My sentiments exactly," I was pleased to agree.

"It is to decorate your house then?"

"Not really! It is my friend's. She had it sitting near a window, the little door always open, and called it her spirit house. I am taking it home with me.

Before I could ask why his friend did not want it any longer, the man surprised me with the question:

"Do you believe in spirits, that they can roam, seek refuge?"

"There is much we do not know or understand, perhaps they exist all around us", I answered.

To talk about spirits with a stranger was unusual and I wondered about the direction the conversation was taking. I had encountered before that strangers in passing on a journey might reveal to each other what they might not otherwise, knowing that with the end of the journey, teller, audience and events just slip into never land. I waited. The man was obviously troubled about something.

As if addressing the endlessly green fields beyond, before the train left them behind, he began:

"I lost my friend. She was of Indian origin and felt that she must visit the land of her ancestors. I wish now I had gone with her! I do not hold much with traveling to uncomfortable strange places. She went with her girl friend. The two traveled from the south to the north of India. They promised to be careful and stay in good hotels. She would send me e-mails or call whenever possible."

"At the beginning of her trip," he went on, "mails told how the poverty, dust and dirt shocked her, beggars haunted her.   Then, she wrote that she enjoyed the food and the bazaars and how colorful and beautiful were garments. She loved the cotton and had been shopping. People crowds everywhere bothered her. She envied the people's simple way of living."

"From her vantage point of a privileged tourist," I added and he smiled.   "She felt strangely at home there."

I nodded. Once I viewed that land and her people, committed to live there. In Calcutta I wore those soft cotton saris, ate Indian food, learned my husband's language and adopted Indian ways. They seemed to have stood the test of time and fitted the environment. But, I too lived a privileged life there, shielded by the man who loved me. I did not tell this to my companion, not wanting to divert from his story.

The man looked at me and beyond me, as he continued.

"She sent postcards of ancient sites and cities, wrote on each one only 'Greetings! Keep this!' and her name. Her e-mails became long traveling reports spiced with her thoughts, each ending with "Please print!"

Mine were long letters then.

Painfully serene seemed the man's face as he continued.

"Last, the two women visited an ancient temple site in South India, by the side of the Bay of Bengal. She called to tell me of snow white sand, turquoise, clean water, slim, black fishermen and women, neat villages huddling behind dunes, warm sea breeze and peaceful village land around. She was happy! She always loved the sea."

The man sat silent, in my mind I revisited where the women had been. As if collecting himself, he went on.

"Her next e-mail told of a strange encounter that troubled her. A palm reader had approached them, offering to read their palms, tell their fate. At first my friend declined, but her companion accepted. When the palm reader told what she knew was true she too presented her hand. The man looked at her palm, she wrote, turned without a word, as if struck and vanished in the crowd without being paid."

I remembered my own experience with a palm reader once, when he shocked me with the truth, that he could not have known.

"The last mail told how simple spirituality touched her. From the hotel balcony she watched a woman come out of the gate of her house with a cup and cloth in hand just after sunrise. Dipping the cloth, she slowly drew a most beautiful white floral onto the concrete entrance floor of her house. The same woman appeared the following morning, washed away what was left of her drawing, and created a new equally beautiful one in its place. My friend saw in it a woman's morning prayer, beautifying her house, soliciting protection and welcoming anyone entering."

"I know them as alpoona' and love them and that tradition," I interjected.

The man had hardly heard me and turned to looking out the window, as if reviewing the land.

"She was to return that following week," he said softly, "instead, there came the call of her death."

"I am so sorry!" I exclaimed. "But how did she die?"

"When she did not appear for breakfast that morning and did not answer, her companion asked her hotel room door to be opened. They found her in bed, her throat cut. The bathroom window was broken. A thin golden chain she used to wear around her neck was missing."

"How horrible! Have they found the murderer?"

The man shook his head.

"Someone sent me a cutting from an Indian newspaper with her picture, which explained that the police was looking for hints and a hotel servant. It was a four-star hotel."

"It was her fate," I said, as if this would take away his pain and explain the horror.

Low automatic lights went on in our compartment as the train rattled noisily through a long tunnel, sound bouncing off the walls, silencing everything else.   Suddenly daylight reappeared; the train resumed its monotonous, rhythmic song.   My companion looked at me.

"I wonder what one knows of one's destiny. Before my friend undertook her journey, she obsessed about the fate of the Alaskan salmon dying at its place of birth. I wonder whether she was drawn to her place of origin to fulfill a destiny."

I nodded and said, "Who really knows about life and death and our time in between, our fate."

The beautiful bird house stood on the seat and I wondered aloud, "Do you believe that her spirit might roam, seek refuge in the bird house?   Considering how she died, and that she called it her spirit house, are you taking it to your home, believing that her spirit might visit?"

"Hers might be a tormented haunted spirit," said the man most sincerely, "if it would comfort, I would want to offer it a place to rest. She believed that what we cannot see still is. Some Catholics have an ever burning candle on the graves of their loved ones. The bird house had an unusual meaning to her; I will set it near a window."

"Will you put water and food into the little containers?"

"I might, it is done, it might be the thought that counts", smiled my companion.

"It comforts body and soul to do something", I added.

"Spirits may not need the open door, but the sparrows would."

Calm companionship settled in our compartment; the sun had set and soon the lights would go on. Shortly, the train slowed, rolled into a station and the man got up. He carefully lifted the bird house. His question on leaving took me by surprise:

"Do you believe in soul mates?"

"Yes, they are of the spirit", I smiled in return. He tilted his head towards me in a friendly farewell nod and I gave him the same. Did he consider me a soul mate in passing or did he refer to his departed dear friend?

The journey home I had taken many times, knowing what a wise old man had told me, once frustrated about another move my husband initiated.

"No place on earth is ever your home."

As the world outside became dark, and dim lights of small stations hurried by, I thought of my own journey, fate, free will, consequences and the truth of "Man proposes, God disposes".

I suppose everyone's journey begins with birth and ends with death. In between are lots of people and events and the question, what makes us decide one way or another.

On the drive from the airport of Calcutta into town, the lines across balconies with clean laundry fluttering in the hot midday breeze, aided by the upward air flow of the chaotic traffic on the roads, were surely the only familiar sight, although the clothing I knew, were six yard long fabric pieces,   saris or dhotis, with a few children' pants and dresses in between. Calcutta was hot and humid in September and it smelled strange.

My hair blew wildly about my face. The taxi's windows were open; its cranks were altogether missing.   The turbaned grimy taxi driver raced, honking wildly, maneuvering from right to left of the road and in between, avoiding collisions with cars and people.

The man next to me secretly stole my hand to hold and press for courage, as I examined his country. I could not have imagined that some years later, I would dare to face this traffic as driver of our car.

Memory is like a swamp where incidents and events stand out like tufts of grass, recalling them, is like walking stepping onto that bit of solid ground. That one Sunday in Calcutta so many years ago, held the promise of an eventfully joyful day. Unknowingly and unintentionally, the participants not even recognizing the extraordinary in the ordinary moment, the direction of our lives changed, in the way a train gets put onto a different track to take it onward to its destiny.

Our marriage was too bold a break with tradition. The family could not accept our union. They needed time to adjust.

So did the world around us in Calcutta. Fires of hurt burnt in hearts, fires from perceived ingratitude, disappointment and fear. Ensuing smoke clouded visions. We went about our lives together my husband and I, watching, learning and understanding.

As working woman of the twenty-first century I observed: my engineer father could accepted his strange son-in-law as fellow engineer, my father-in-law accepted his foreign daughter-in-law out of love and respect for his son and because of the father she had. I wondered whether this satisfied a suitable, although different gene pool. As generations before, I puzzled, the men jointly entrusted to their less educated woman their family welfare and the upbringing of their children, assuming that respectful consideration to all ancestral backgrounds was guaranteed. The women knew, would watch this new foreign family member.

Out stands another eventful Sunday in Calcutta. Sugar and flour were rationed at that time and dependent on the most vulnerable availability of electricity it was no small accomplishment that I had succeeded to bake a good cake in my luxurious German oven to welcome my father-in-law, coming in on the train.

Grandfather came to see his new granddaughter. He blessed her with a gift of a rare golden coin for her wealth and happiness, and she blessed him with wet from her diaper to my great embarrassment and his amusement. We were called out of our siesta by the clatter of something falling onto the kitchen floor and saw to our amazement a never before seen monkey escape through the kitchen window with part of my cake in hand. On the same day came the new servant who endlessly ironed dry the baby's cloth diapers.

Such incidents of life seem like games that imps like to play with humans. But I learned also to recognize the guardian angels that intercept fate on our behalf. On my lunch brake I came out of a familiar side road to stop before entering the wild traffic of Calcutta's main street, the 4 to 5 lanes without any lines between then. The brakes on my car failed just there and then, the brake pedal had snapped, my foot hit void. I remember cars zooming past me, a taxi cut a wide curve in front of me, and I had shot straight across onto the small park lane without a scratch.

From that day on I argued that guardian angels direct traffic and even the best driver better have one.

Those helpers of fate come as ordinary and extraordinary people, as if they were unobtrusive soul mates to protect or redirect our journey on this earth. India has an impressive monkey, silver gray, with black markings on face, hands and feet and a long tail, he sits 4 feet tall.

An Indian epic tells how the king of those monkeys with his monkey army brought back an Indian queen, who was held hostage by an ogre on what is now the island of Sri Lanka. Those monkeys remain revered in India and often befriend priests of temples. When my husband was a baby, the family relates, his mother visited a temple with him. A monkey stole the baby from her and to her horror carried him to the upper-ledges of the temple. A priest who knew the monkey tempted him down with a bunch of bananas for which he safely gave back the baby.

One day my husband decided to leave India for the United States. Was it a stubborn self reliance, the desire to better his family or did he just take the opportunity of the times and the promises it held? I wonder what we instinctively might know of our path and fate. It seems we always were in the place where his heart could be saved, by science and by people.

Immigrants of earlier days seldom had the opportunity to connect with their homelands to reinforce a cultural base and values and incorporate inevitable changes. Those immigrants simply integrated into American life and molded it. At our time, the world began to shrink with planes and information highways across the globe. Our family enjoyed the mixed blessing of a three cultural balance act. We were neither completely German, nor Indian, nor what we perceived as American. We visited India and Germany, connecting with families who came to visit us.

I remained a woman with accent, together my husband and I always stood out. Our names, our appearance, our mannerism confused and intrigued people. We were watched and so were our children. Reference to our little daughter, stubborn as all Germans, made me realize that in this nation of cultures, identifying people by categorizing them was just convenient. In reality the human race was no different than our little family;   one had only to go back far enough in the history of mankind to see that there were always strangers in strange lands who changed cultures and got changed themselves. We were just moving onward, not knowing where it would lead us and why.

The India I lived in was not the tourist India, but the real middle class India.   A little girl who had never seen a white woman close up sat next to me one day stroking my arm.   I realized, she thought, I was powdered white and surely it would come of. We both laughed, we both learned.

Calcutta was less crowded and fear of people I did not know.   Years later I realized what danger and liability I was to my husband's people.   They had experiences with hungry, despairing, angry, hostile, and dangerous crowds that I could not understand. On a family excursion one of two cars broke down. It was dark at 6 p.m. My husband and I were with great urgency ushered into the working car with children and the driver sped away. I stood out, they attracted attention.   A dangerous area where a killing mob is easily ignited, I was told, and they knew to protect me and themselves.   That an Indian   truck driver was rescued by police that day from death by a quickly forming   mob, because, on the almost impassable narrow roads filled with people, he had   hit, but not killed, a man on his bicycle and knocked down an electric pole,   plunging the area in darkness for days, demonstrated their point.

Good people there and everywhere do what they can and where they cannot, they pray and hold candlelight vigils. I am still the only foreigner in my Indian family, but not the only woman chosen out of love. The time had come for such change, but we were surprised what teaching had come through us. On a most enjoyable visit to India, as guest of my husband's favorite brother, we played bridge one day with the parents of his son's wife. The mother of the bride confessed that she vehemently opposed her daughter's choice of husband because he was of different cast, from another Indian state, spoke a different Indian language and was not a vegetarian. She would and could not give her blessing to such a union, would not permit the wedding.

My husband's brother came to talk and asked her to accept his son, as he would accept her daughter because of the love the two had for each other to spare herself of the sadness he once had encountered on our behalf.

On this she gave her blessing and the wedding took place. She was glad she did and wanted us to know what change we had brought about.

Darkness had fallen on the land outside my window and with excitement I began to watch out for the faint lights and names of small stations. The old familiar station lay in almost darkness when I stepped of the train.

The platform and tunnel under the tracks looked shabbier and dirtier than I remembered and the neon lights in the station hall glared strangely.

Memories of India and the bird house sank back into the swamp of the mind. I was 'home' in the place and with the people of my old world. There is something joyful about a familiar place. I knew my path out of the station towards a taxi, as I knew the palm of my hand. The taxi took the new road. New is inevitable, it is good.

Writer's Wish

Closed the journal
intended
words no more invented
imprisoned on a page
indifference, joy, rage,

give to the wind
to whip about
throw into a cloud
of lightening and thunder
roar

rain wash it under
compost it all
fermented
good and bad
as equal rise on call.

It has long been known that the pen is mightier than the sword. This gives me many reasons for writing. To name a few: to explore people, places and things; to share and record thoughts; to entertain; as an outlet for depression; and as a challenge to stimulate my creativity are among the more important.

I can invent characters based on my moods much like when I was a child and played pretend because there was no one else to play with. Through my writing I can have as many friends as I want; be whoever I want. Kings and queens in far off lands would not be out of my reach.

Traveling to Paris to have breakfast, tea in London or dining by the Sea of Tranquility sounds like fun if I so desire. I can shop for a new wardrobe; escape to lands no one has ever heard of; attend Harvard Law School--graduating with honors to say the least. All of this can be had without spending a dime.

Perhaps, I'll entertain a different lover everyday of the week-- with some of the choices I've had, that's about how long each relationship would last, I think. It is possible to have one be a beast, another a saint or maybe just an ordinary guy. Spending the day with Brad Pitt may be some gal's dream, but I think Paul Newman would be more interesting. The one person that has always intrigued me was Yul Bryner. His eyes could pierce one's very soul. Then, too, I remember the nights I would lie awake thinking of running my fingers through his hair. Thank goodness there were not too many of them.

Did you know that it is possible to win the lottery, solve the entire world's problems, bring people back to life, heal the sick or change history just with the stroke of my pen or by pressing a few buttons on my computer? Adding humor to my writing can cheer me up; mystery can give me a challenge--maybe even bumping off my ex--now that's something to get excited about.

Let's see, how should I do it? Guns are too noisy; those swords or knives are too messy. I've got it, one of the same ways he tried to get rid of me. I'll lure him into a field of rattle snakes--I'll have to make some kind of deal with the rattlesnakes so they won't bite me.

What can I use for trade? They wouldn't have any use for money. So, I'll offer food and protection for the rest of their lives-

-that should do it. I'll have to think more about setting this up. Murder can be so much fun and with no consequences.

Another thing I thoroughly enjoy about writing is winning any argument, because I can always have the last word. I'll bet you think I live in fantasy land, so what? Sometimes the fantasy world helps one survive the horrors of the real world. However, I do know when to come back to earth, and that is as soon as I shut off my computer. But after all, my writing world is my world, and I can make magic happen in any form I choose.

Flirtation

To such malarkey,
Ladies listen.
Worker whistles,
Compliment.
Hair and skin
In sun, glistens
Spirits lifted,
Heaven sent.

The Big Heist

The only time I ever ran out of gas was in the middle of a big heist. I was on my way home when my car loaded down with stolen goods died from thirst.

It was getting late and I walked back down the street to the place I had just picked up the goods. I told the guys I needed some gas.

I'm sure they thought I must be the most stupid person on earth. That should be the first thing you think of—a full tank of gas for the getaway. I didn't tell them I had never done a getaway before; but they knew it.

Well, the guys only had a little gas to perhaps get me to a service station. I was crossing the four-lane highway to the only open station I could see. Again, right in the middle of the highway, the '67 Chevy Impala coughed, sputtered and died. Two lanes of cars were flying low straight at me at about fifty miles an hour.

It was dark. I immediately started flashing my lights and blowing my horn to get their attention. I could just see the headlines in the morning paper— Woman Killed in Getaway.

It really wasn't the cops I was afraid of. I had my car full of what I knew to be community property. Frank and I were going through a divorce, and he kept taking property off to his relatives to hide it. I told the judge that we had a garage full of equipment that totaled about $75,000. The judge, Frank's lawyer, and even my lawyer shook their heads in disbelief. They were sure I didn't know what I was talking about. They didn't say this, but it was implied by their tone. They did say that there was no way that we had that kind of property based on our income.

"But he stole it out of the schools," I said. They continued to shake their heads and look at me as if I was nuts. Frank told them he had about $2,000 worth of tools and some of them weren't even his. They belonged to a couple of his friends. He went to the trouble to get his friends to lie about it and write a letter stating which items belonged to them; that was a crime also. The judge and lawyers all believed the lies he was telling.

On the next day, I went to work and told a co-worker my problem. She said, "Well, if he can do it, so can you."

"Of course," I agreed. "But I don't have a place to put it, nor can I possibly lift it." There was lots of big machinery involved.

"I know someone who will do it for you," she said excitedly.

So, a few days later it was raining. I went to work. Frank went to work. And the guys went to work. Because of the weather, most people would be staying inside and not question what was going on at our house even though our neighbors knew we weren't home. They would think it was Frank's brothers over there, working in my husband's shop. The guys backed the black van up to the garage and loaded it up and drove off. Again and again this went on all day long.

By the time school was out, the guys were done. A four and a half car drive-through garage full of lathes, welders, big saws, milling machines, drill presses, an air compressor and just about anything you could think of was somewhere else. The attic over the garage had been full also, and its contents were gone. Every nook and cranny was empty--every screw, every nail—all gone.

When Frank came home, he walked into the garage. I wish I could have seen the expression on his face when he opened the garage door. It would have been a sight worth a million dollars. He let out a holler of expletives which I wouldn't repeat. When he came back into the house, I could hardly keep a straight face. He started raving about the mafia coming and stealing all his stuff out of the garage. It was a big job, and he thought only the mafia could have pulled it off in the allotted time.

I wasn't expecting him to do what he did next; after all, he had stolen most of the stuff from vocational schools where he worked. However, it was exactly what I wanted and desperately needed. He called the police.

I was in the garage with Frank and the police; I had to run outside because I was about to bust my gut with laughter especially when he told them what it was worth. The police made out a report of $75,000 worth of equipment stolen out of the garage. I went back into the house because I couldn't keep from laughing.

A few minutes later, one of the detectives came inside to use the phone. I couldn't look him in the eye. My grin would have given me away immediately. I was glad when he went back outside. I called the guys that had pulled the job. "Hey, did you guys use gloves? The police think that stuff might have gone across the river and are notifying the FBI."

This I made up because I knew the stuff had to go back into the garage. It was the only way I could scare those guys into putting it all back. After all, I had my report.

The next day I told the police that I pulled the job. I explained to them why I did it and knew it had to go back. They had never heard tell of such a thing, but they got a good laugh out of it. It was only one of two times that I got the best of Frank. The other was a very minor thing.

Frank didn't believe in insurance.   After our divorce, I found out the house wasn't even insured except for the amount of the original loan. Anyway, none of the stuff was insured. The only crime involved was when my husband filed the police report. After all I had just as much right to it as he did and he was hauling it all off himself. What's the difference, right?

Well, according to the property laws, Frank could haul it off right in front of me and there was nothing I could do about it. The police had made many trips to our house because of his abuse to me and the kids. They knew Frank was a mean guy. Our lives were in constant danger from this man.

Getting the stuff back in the garage was really tricky. We had to get it all back before Frank came home to keep the guys from getting shot. I had seen my husband shoot someone before. It was one of his students, and he got away with it. Frank didn't kill the kid, but the doctors couldn't remove the bullet from his head because of the location. Frank said he shot him just for the heck of it.   His punishment was a promotion from teacher to principal.

All the neighbors were peeping from their windows because Detective Barnes had been around talking to them about what they had seen the day before. My daughter, Gina was the lookout while they were putting the stuff back.

Every time Gina saw headlights come around the corner, she would yell, "Dad's coming!"

This was so hysterically funny that I was laughing so hard I could hardly stand up. They would drop everything, jump the fence and take off--leaving the truck as it was. Then the lookout would yell, "False alarm!"

They would return and work faster than before. Their only means of transportation was the truck. They had to get it emptied before Frank got home. It was down to just a few items.   The lookout yelled, "Dad's coming!" This was really taking a toll on those guys.

"You're gonna have to come over and get the rest of this stuff in your car tomorrow. All the big and heavy stuff is back," said one of the guys.

When Frank came home, he went out and looked in the garage. It was like he had had a nightmare. He came into the house, "Its all back." It was not organized like it had been before, but he didn't say anything about this.

"Well, maybe the mafia had a guilty conscience." Then I told him I did it.   Frank's mouth dropped open—he could hardly believe this. He acquired a new found respect for me after that. I also told him that the board of education had been out in the garage looking at the stuff too.   Some was still in crates marked board of education and worth thousands. This scared him. Sometime during the night those things disappeared.

The court date in our divorce came up, and I had the report. The judge lit into him for lying about the stuff. Frank was trying to take everything; I knew I had three kids to support and was not about to let him get away with this. So, I got the house, and he got his equipment plus all the hidden bank accounts, stocks, and other stuff.

After our divorce was final, Frank left most of the items in the garage.   My co-worker told me that burgling was a regular thing for the guys, but they had given it up at least for a while.

When I started experimenting with words, writing became a game for me. My first love of the written word came from my mother. I watched her diligence in reading and writing. After I started school, my family moved frequently, so my early school experiences are vague. I remember my seventh grade teacher helping my class memorize several poems. At that time, I did not realize the impact these poems would have on my life. I still recall certain lines from poems. The memorized poems have served as a source of inspiration for my own poems.

Once I started teaching reading in school, I started writing poetry and stories. On weekends and weeknights, I spent my leisure hours writing. After my school supervisor discovered my interest in writing, she encouraged me to share my work with others.

Writing provided me with a medium of expression I enjoyed. While I taught school, I spent time reading other people's writings. Materials I read, along with my earlier experiences, had a profound influence over my life. I felt compelled to write. In my writings, I wanted people to laugh, cry, or learn something.

My experiences in teaching children and adults helped me discover the power of the printed page. Reading materials I used taught concepts; the books showed children different aspects of their own makeup, too. During the reading process, I saw children develop listening, language, writing, and social skills. After retiring from a full-time teaching career, I have attempted to create clean-cut educational and recreational reading materials for people to enjoy.

Over a period of years, I have shared my work with children and adults. In the future, I want to use anecdotes, experiences, travel, and religion as fodder for other poems or books.

Goldilocks: Twenty Years Later

Walking through the woods isn't on my agenda any longer. Since the day I faced three bears, I haven't returned to the lovely cottage in the woods. Trying out the bears' chairs, sampling their porridge, and sleeping in Baby Bear's bed made me happy. But my heart leaped from my torso when I awoke and saw three bears. I, Goldilocks, sped away like a racing horse, never returning to the cottage again.

Of course, entering a city like Atlanta has its own bears, too. I'm not speaking of furry bears with fierce teeth. I'm talking about frightening experiences, causing you to retreat to a more comfortable environment.

Don't get me wrong. I like to go out with my friends. On one particular night, Rita and I decided to take my new set of wheels, commonly called my baby, to Atlanta. We chose to leave the convertible top down to enjoy the scenery. Seeing the sunset over the Olympic Park made the trip worthwhile. Rita and I "oohed" and "aahed" about its beauty, and we chatted about other cool spots. While I drove, I convinced Rita of the fun we'd have at the planetarium.

I remember Rita saying, "I guess we could take it in. Let's check out the Varsity and the guys first." Then she brushed her hair into a loose ponytail to keep it from slapping her face.

I replied, "Later in the evening, we could go dancing at a new place in Atlanta. Several students from my college graduation class plan to be there."

"Yeah, I'd like that," she replied.

When I pulled into the Varsity, Rita checked out her surroundings. "Would you get my hamburger and fries while I get us a table?" she asked me.

Even though I wanted to check things out myself, I agreed to get the food.

After I received our order and got to the table, many friends and strangers sat or stood in close proximity to Rita. Her easygoing style and gift of gab attracted both men and women.

I sat down beside Rita and enjoyed the company. When it was time to leave, we grabbed our belongings and paid our bill.

Once we arrived at the planetarium, we found a seat and admired the constellations. I couldn't remember the names of all of them, but the Big Dipper, the Little Dipper, and the bear-shaped one fascinated me. I admit that the bear-shaped constellation brought back bygone memories. I didn't dwell on my frightening experience with the bears, though. Instead, I focused on our next adventure.

"Are we going dancing, now?" Rita inquired.

"We're on our way. I'm not much of a dancer, though," I said.

"You'll get the hang of it. You're probably better than 90% of the dancers in here," Rita said with an encouraging tone."

After I learned a few steps, I liked dancing with my friends. When I checked the time later, I knew we needed to leave. Rita didn't want to go, but she gathered her purse, and we headed out.

On the way home, Rita and I chatted about our evening. Before long, our ride home changed from what I'd envisioned. A sound I didn't like came from the hood of my new car. I pulled off the road. While I got out, Rita grabbed her cell phone. As she dialed for help, I screamed. My eyes saw a bear standing ahead of me. Would I be eaten? I wondered.

Rita jumped back into the car. Her eyes searched the backseat for anything to scare the bear away. She kept one eye on the backseat and one eye on me.

Once I looked into the bear's face, I could imagine the bear gobbling me up for supper. My fear subsided when I gazed into the bear's eyes again. The bear looked at me as if she recognized me. Her mouth closed and for no apparent reason, she wandered off. Quickly, I adjusted a cable under the car hood. When I tried the car again, it started without any other problems.

Rita was numb, but she managed to speak, as I drove onto the road. She asked, "Goldilocks, how did you tame the bear? I thought you didn't like bears after your last encounter with them twenty years ago."

"Bears do scare me. The bear I saw tonight was a grown-up version of Baby Bear. She recognized me. I felt like she was a long lost friend."

"You're lucky that she wasn't hungry. I wouldn't trust any bear," Rita said.

"I guess bears are somewhat like men. They prey on other creatures for food and wants. Tonight, we didn't become a meal ticket for anyone. I think it pays to be friendly to other creatures, but I'll still choose my friends carefully," I said.

"I will too," Rita said. "I enjoyed the evening. Thanks for being a good friend." Then she stepped onto the sidewalk and disappeared into her residence.

Being Thankful

I'm thankful for the small things
Surrounding me, each and every day.
And for the gift of life,
As I approach each hour;
I live my life to the fullest,
Until Jesus carries me home.

I'm grateful for God's creatures,
And for children's winning smiles.
I relish a friendly hello,
To brighten up my day.
I enjoy my dog's coy tricks,
Causing chuckles to spill from within.

I'm thankful for rays of color
Surrounding me outside.
I pause to revel in the sights
And let the beauty stir my soul
That comes from my master's paintbrush,
Created especially for me.

I'm grateful for musical tones,
Which delightfully strike my ears.
They engulf my soul from within
With warm and dissonant sounds.
The tones create rhythms and moods
And inspire my walk on life's path.

Untitled

Flowers
Lovely, sweet smells,
Standing, swaying, swishing
Visually appeal to my eyes
Blossoms.

Untitled

A patient bridegroom
Waits at the altar,
A shimmering light appears.

"Why don't you use your talent to write something someone can use? You should write self-help books like Doctor Phil. You're wasting your gift on these made-up stories. You could make a real difference in the world if you wrote about something real."

While promoting my new novel, I was amazed by the many comments insinuating that fiction writing a waste of effort. Is it truly wasting my talent by spending time in front of a computer making up stories about people who would have been long dead even if they had really existed in the first place?

I seriously began to question if I should want to write fiction. Writing is hard work. The hardest part might be when work is unrecognized and unappreciated. Why bother with all this aggravation? Maybe I should simply spend more time with my family and less in the fantasy world.

One night I determined I would break the habits of a lifetime. I would put the pen down. No more writing! I would read something truly worthwhile. I opened my favorite book, the Bible. To my astonishment, I instantly found myself engulfed in a wealth of fiction stories told by the greatest storyteller of all time. I enjoyed anew the stories of the persistent widow, the prodigal son and of the unfaithful servants in the vineyard. Never before had I considered the idea that the parables might be fictional stories.

I wondered why Jesus had not simply stood up and preached to the crowd as he had on the Sermon on the Mount. Why had he not boldly insisted on his will, as when he chased the moneychangers from the Temple? Why had he resorted to storytelling to get these messages to his audience?

Then the idea struck me that maybe he realized that the issue cannot be forced. Attention must be caught and listeners entertained before they will truly hear what is being said. And Jesus certainly knew how to reach the dullest audience. If Jesus seemed to feel that telling a fictional story was a valid path for reaching others, who was I to doubt his methods?

I admit that there certainly is a lot of wasteful, empty fiction in existence, but maybe that sad fact should challenge authors to go out and create stories of compelling interest that can also be of great value to society. The next time someone suggests that I write something someone can really use, I intend to hand them one of my made-up stories and assure them I am seriously making the effort to do just that.

Music On The Wind

As a young girl I would stand out in my front lawn and listen to the sound of piano and flute floating with the wind to my house. Since I was just a scraggly kid with perpetually skinned knees, I was never invited inside my sophisticated neighbors' house for a private concert. I had to settle for enjoying the music from a distance.

Those talented neighbors moved away, and even without the pleasure of those charming duets, I retained my profound infatuation with music. That love stayed with me as I grew to be a teenager.

Like most adolescent girls, I fell in love. Unfortunately, I was smitten with a severe case of unrequited love. The boy I adored was popular and good looking. He was also the one wonderful thing in my existence that kept me from dwelling on the awful turmoil of my home life.

The object of my worship occupied the chair next to me in band class. We would pass silly notes or leave them for one another on our shared music stand. Somehow I was christened with the nickname "Doo Lolly." Only we knew the meaning behind this private joke.

One afternoon his chair was empty. My classmates were spreading the hot rumor that he had quit band. No explanation. And worse, there had been no goodbye.

Like so many other times in my life, the idea was reinforced that I was a nobody. I was not worth a second thought. I did not even rate a simple farewell. I decided I was always going to stand on the outside listening to music on the wind.

I was so upset by this sudden catastrophe that I could not hear a note the band was playing. I slumped low in my seat and hoped I did not catch the band director's notice. I felt as if my ears were stuffed with cotton. I did not want to hear the music. I hated the music. I hated everything! I made the effort to play my contrabass but it was like a cactus full of prickly splinters when I put the reed against my tongue. I wanted to cover my ears, crawl into a hole and be left alone in my misery.

Just leave me alone to die!

Through the blur of threatening tears, I caught sight of a slip of paper poking out of the edge of my music folder. Notebook paper did not belong in a world of pure white sheet music with black ink notes.

I stopped pretending I was playing my horn and just stared. Red ink bled through the paper. I always wrote my notes in red ink, an adolescent statement that I might be writing my passionate, fervent thoughts in my own blood.

Then I realized this message was placed on his side of the music stand. With trembling hands, I slowly turned the paper over. Many months earlier I had written him some foolish letter and he had used that same piece of paper to scratch out a hurried note.

Nothing elegant. Nothing poetic. But those brief words in his sprawling handwriting dug deep into my soul.

"I'll miss Doo Lolly."

Away flew the disappointment that our friendship would never blossom into romance. What was important was this heartfelt admission that I was worthy of his time and his friendship. The little girl, who always felt so inconsequential and been left on the outside to hear the duet on the wind, had finally heard the lyrical notes of acceptance.

The ride on the school bus did not seem so long that afternoon. I clasped that piece of paper in my hand the entire way home. For once in my life I found it easy to ignore the bullies who always took issue with my contrabass blocking the aisle. The horn did not even seem very heavy as I lugged the large instrument along the street.

My steps slowed as I passed the house where my neighbors had once played their piano and flute concerts. I stopped, unable to believe what I was hearing. An old familiar melody trailed across the lawn to the curb where I lingered.

I took a long, cautious look around me then studied every detail of that house. All was dark with no lights shining from the windows. No one was home. Who was playing this music? And how did these new neighbors know this particular piece? That they had a record of the exact song the former occupants use to play seemed an incredible coincidence.

I leaned my chin on the tall contrabass case and puzzled and wondered. I puzzled and wondered some more. Then I finally realized where the music originated. The music was coming from inside me.

I think that was the moment in my life that I realized there would always be music…

poetry…
　books…
　　grand, noble thoughts…
　　　long, lingering sunsets…
　　　　and good, lasting friendships…

as long as I claimed them and called them my own.
All those grand, fine joys and gifts that made life so
brilliant and worthwhile would only be mine if I
reached out and embraced them. I could not expect
them to simply drift my way like music on the wind.

I would have to close my ears to the nay-sayers,
the bullies, and even to the fathers who did not
understand my dreams. I accepted the fact that this
would be a lifelong fight, maybe always uphill and
desperate, but I made a pledge to myself at that
moment that I would ardently pursue the music and all
those wonders that make life so magical and
worthwhile.

SARAH JANE DE LUCA

My reasons for writing have changed over the decades.

I received a five year diary from my mother and father on my tenth birthday. Its pages were bound in soft red leather, secured by a small gold lock that opened with a tiny key. The diary invited my secrets, and I recorded them every night for the next five years. They were small offerings, of course; the diary allowed only a couple of inches of writing space for each entry. My writing was crabbed and tight. Sometimes I didn't have a lot to say. There are a few dates that are totally bereft of detail, saying simply: Lousy day.

But the great, expansive days, the quiet days, yes, even the lousy days – a child is allowed to have some of those - rolled by more quickly than I could have imagined possible. And the little diary was filled with milestones and memories that spilled over the allotted inches, into its margins. The journaling habit was well established. At fifteen, I graduated to thick, college-ruled notebooks that would allow me to write at much as I wished. I continued to write almost daily, because I needed to, not simply because there was an allocated space that asked me to account for my days. I wrote to discover what I was feeling and thinking.

"How can I know what I think until I see what I say?" That quote by E.M. Forster describes my primary motivation for recording my life, beginning in adolescence, and continuing through my middle years. I expanded my format beyond the journal – moving into memoir, short story, poetry. I fell in love with the rhythm and music of words, and the challenge of arranging them in artful sequence. I fell in love with the telling details that add up to story and enable people to connect with each other's truth and experience.

When I became a grandmother, at the age of fifty-five, my writing seemed to take on additional purpose. I want my grandchildren to understand their history, their deep identity. Now I write for them – for their children, and for their children's children. I want to help them realize how time and place molds and shapes us, and conversely, how very constant human nature remains, across culture and across the centuries. Such understanding leads to tolerance; tolerance is the foundation of peace.

And so I continue to take measure of my days. I convert my truth into story, using the written word to connect with a time I can not know.

Braiding Dandelions

We find a wild, prolific crop of dandelions
splashing the vacant lot behind my mother's house.
When I was young – about your age –
my mother says to Emma, eight years old –
I braided crowns and necklaces from flowers.
These dandelions should work just fine –
Now watch!

She breaks off several milky stems –
some long and close to ground,
some midway,
others stubby, inches from the bloom.

The trick, my artist-mother says,
is to work three stems at a time, all different lengths.
When one runs out
you splice a new one in its place; that way
you never break the chain.

Emma plops down in the deep wet grass.
I kneel between the generations.
We laugh at rough beginnings, ragged endings,
but we persevere. We practice,
practice till we get it right, Emma, Mom and me,
our heads bent low,
lost in a field of yellow tassels.

When our circles hold.
We rise
and crown each other with our handiwork.

The Cows Are Out

Our mother's agitated voice
rides on the dawn, at milking time:
Quick kids! We need your help!
The cows are out!

We stagger up from patchwork sleep,
pull on stiff overalls and shirts and shoes,
fly down to meet the dreaded task.
The cause is clear - a skittish heifer
stormed the new electric fence, crashed through.
Now, spiked with energy,
she leads a dozen bawling sisters
on a wild tour of Mama's garden

Freedom confounds them.
They churn excitedly across the rows,
trampling the cabbages, bell peppers, tall tomatoes,
ripping pea vines, bringing the cornstalks down.

My sisters and I know our moves:
arms splayed like scarecrows, we fan out,
we sing and shout,
press toward the barnyard gate, surround,
surround. Our mother coaxes and cajoles –
come boss, come boss –
while Daddy's wild curses spook the cattle
and move kids to prayer –
please God, please help us get them in.
The Holsteins stall and shift and shy,
go off ten maddened ways, then somehow
gain some sense and stumble home.

Weak-kneed, we climb the stairs to bed,
sink down to sleep, dampened

by sweat and dew and breath of cows,
charged with electric dreams.

Grounding

I never saw the ocean as a child
but felt instead the inland tides
of morning chores and evening chores
and all the tasks that fell between those shores –
the splash of milk from pail to strainer
and the frothy rising and the draining down
inside the can.

I felt the tug of duty from a stone boat
crossing a sea of new-turned soil. A season later
grasses lured me, waving green and all together,
rooted singly, planted deep. When snow descended
I was called by sheep and cattle
and I ferried hay across the banks and barriers,
always eagerly received.

Sometimes I wondered at the town kids,
thinking they must drift like snowflakes,
light and free, without the careful watch
of time and weather. They must feel loose as seeds
caught in a summer wind,
without the heaving patch of earth
that anchored me.

Splicing the Rope

There would be little rest for any crewman
on a 1950's haying day,
little respite from the growling tractors, hissing heat,
blue dust of stem and leaf baled tight,
the bite of twinestring,
sharp and throbbing through thick leather gloves.

My father liked to work the mow,
shielded from engines, shouting men and grinding
sun.
He smiled to see the iron spider crawl its web
with eight dense bales gripped fast in its forked legs –
up, up –
enjoyed the twisting, groaning of the rope,
the hesitation of a swiveling cargo at the open peak,
the quaking pulley and the running in across a fast,
straight track –
Whoa! Trip 'er! – the resulting din,
the bouncing bricks of baked alfalfa at his feet.

The now man didn't seem to mind
hefting those heavy bales, straining to keep the pace,
smoothing the cliffs and caverns of his dim domain.
He also called the halt, perhaps too joyfully,
each time a hayrope frayed or broke,
for he could sit then and create a great, long splice.
He made fine craft of it, a braid so perfect
that it took on meaning of its own.
Quite lost in this, we worked with naked, nimble
fingers
and an artist's attitude, until a crewman called
My gawd, what's going on up there?
We're ready with another load!

Finished or not, he had to let his masterpiece go
down
to meet the test.
It came up strong and steady, bearing the weight,
again,
again,
again.

Publicly confessing a compulsion is never pretty, but therein lies the truth. When I am writing, the physical world begins to peripherally haze and I enter The Zone. Writing in The Zone is more than just minutely addictive. It becomes an altered state of just "being." While my meditative skills seem to be eternally immature, writing in a sense creates a level of meditation. But that is not the heart of it. There is a moment when I have strung a row of words together that creates a powerful and meaningful message that I am compelled to share with the world. And it is not just any words that create that message, but words that flow easily and lovingly in the mind or over the tongue like the most delicately delicious dessert. When I know I have it right, the endorphin rush that follows is what leads to the compulsion to return to write again and again.

The Golden Sapphires of Spring

It all began in the stark, cold stillness of utter aloneness. Actually, I was not really alone. I did have my heart dog, Moonie, a hairless dog that I adore. And it wasn't the kind of aloneness typically associated with the despair of loneliness.

It began simply enough in that time and space when as an adult we have finally nurtured and tendered wisdom into a bud that boldly begins to blossom. It began in the long months following a bitter and omnipresent divorce from a man bent on seeing me and my children harmed and homeless. That wasn't your typical unpleasant divorce, and my perception isn't the typical distortion of a woman scorned. I promise. This divorce had a subtle subliminal undercurrent of malevolence that awakens me, years later, in a cold sweat from the dreams that occasionally haunt me still. No matter how horrific the events that transpired during that time, what emerged and remains today is the calming presence of strength reinforced through survival.

I don't mind being alone any more than I mind being in the comfortable company of those I love. Being alone is easy. It's loneliness that can be excruciating, while being alone is quietly delicious. And it was in a sustained period of being alone that I began an affair with my computer. It, too, started out simply enough. First it was searching the internet for pertinent and useless information. Then bargain hunting. Then chat lists with other hairless dog fanciers. And finally the plunge into the online singles scene.

Keep in mind I never did and still do not want to be one of "those" people. I certainly wouldn't write a story about it if I were. I wouldn't commit to paper the disturbing confession of one of "those" people so sad that they can't find a date, even in the meat market mentality of the bar scene. And I definitely wouldn't want people to confuse me with the demented internet cruisers who find themselves addicted to adult sites.

No, this was different. I promise. This was just an interesting way to meet people from all parts of the world. And admittedly, there was the air of d-a-n-g-e-r, because the warnings of online psychos saturate talk shows daily. I consoled myself that this was different, because this singles site was a Christian site. I also would staunchly insist that I didn't intend to actually find a date; I was just looking for pen pals. I would have insisted, that is, had I actually ever confessed to anyone about such private computer activities at the time.

In all fairness, I did meet many amazing people, as well as several jerks, from this adventure. I even met one of the jerks in person. Mostly I met a handful of pen pals and maintained email correspondence with many of them for years. It should be known that my most pleasant online friends were from Ireland. Just like virtually everyone in America, I love the Irish. In addition, I can claim and prove my Irish heritage. Occasionally they would send pictures of the area in which they lived or worked. More often they told stories of their lives, and I devoured them silently with my own version of an Irish accent.

Some of these pen pals cycled into and out of my life intermittently like seasons of the year. Nearly all of us dated other people that we'd met both online and at the grocery store nearby. We shared our lives and loves and woes online with each other. And when a new relationship would grow more serious and demand more of our attention, we would understandably cease communications for awhile. We typically usually returned when the new had waned, or worse, when our new love was gone.

One of my favorite friends actually stayed in contact for over two years. By then our friendship had successfully endured distance, arguments, and other romances. More notably, our friendship was strongly significant because under the cloak of anonymity we more easily shared the deeper parts of our hearts more commonly reserved for just a couple of people throughout a lifetime. He had grown up with a deep love and appreciation for all things American that championed my love of the Irish. In exchange for trivial stories from my life and times in these United States, he shared events of The Troubles in Northern Ireland.

It was nearly Thanksgiving when he suddenly suggested he should give me a call. This was a prospect far more frightening than it was exciting. After all, this was an overt invasion into my aloneness and not nearly as incognito as online chats or emails. So of course I had only one obvious answer: I gave him my phone number.

Now, I'm an old woman, well at least on the inside. I have been a single mother of two girls with serious disabilities far longer than married. My support systems have been few, and life has more often than not left me weary. There really are so few things that elicit a tiny pitter-patter in my heart these days. After all, it was a quick, ten-minute conversation, and he had a steady girlfriend. I had no business entertaining anything even vaguely resembling pitter-patter. However, the Irish accent dangling at the distant end of the line did the dance.

Sadly, it wasn't long before I had a ghastly realization. It became mandatory that I remove myself from this situation. The only option more ghastly would have been to remain and consequentially come between a man and a woman who were contemplating marriage. So, in just one conversation I found myself not alone but intensely lonely instead. Favorite songs both old and new took on profound meaning, and I sang long and loudly in the depth of my loneliness during each and every drive. My world became clouded under deep shades of gray, and I longed for what had never even been mine. I missed my friend. And my computer, once so compelling and entertaining, became a bitter saboteur. Each new day brought the silence I knew was the only correct choice to make.

Until one day there came a card in my forlorn email inbox:

Teardrops on a rose,
as I stand here all alone.
The fragrance is so sweet
but not for me to own.

You are so far away,
my tears are falling free.
Teardrops on a rose,
please send your love to me.

I see this rose of red,
like drops of blood that fall.
The rose of pink is sweet
like teardrops I recall.

The rose of white, so pure,
yet fragile in its innocence.
Still it opens wide,
so queenly in its elegance.

Teardrops on a rose,
I look to stars above.
Teardrops on a rose,
I long for you, my love.

Michelle: I will never forget you, and I know I will be in your life forever. I love you too much to let you go. I can't get you out of my head, and I don't want to lose that. Love you, Gary.

The next day brought the following:

My love for you is so strong. My nights are long. Since you have been gone, I miss our love we used to share. My heart's not the same since you've gone. I lay awake at night thinking of all the love we shared. I miss you so very much. I pray that you will come back. I miss you as the days go by. Without you here I realize just what you mean to me. And how much I love you. You are my life, my world, my everything. I miss you!

Michelle, I am so sorry if I caused you any more pain. One day I will take that pain away. Gary.

And so it was. With honest integrity, he broke ties with his long-distance girlfriend and wished her well as he bid his farewell. At once his intentions were unilaterally toward me, and my aloneness was about to take another beating. He shortly thereafter announced he was making flight reservations for Easter vacation.

What do you wear to the airport to meet someone in person for the first time that you've known for nearly three years, someone that you know you love even though you've never so much as shared a meal or touched his hand? What do you do when first you meet? Hug? Shake hands? Awkwardly look away? Only in movies sappier than our heretofore story would the script demand we stare knowingly into each other's eyes and then kiss romantically to the background crescendo of an invisible orchestra. There can hardly be many moments in life as surreal as was this. In truth, we were not even sure if we would recognize each other.

First and foremost, I settled for my most flattering pants and a soft, feminine blouse. I also settled for a pillar next to a large plant on the far side of baggage claim so I could assess the situation at my leisure. I knew him the instant I saw him, even though he was remarkably different than the referenced image of him in my mind's eye. And he was shorter than I had envisioned. A lot shorter. But there he was: my past, present, and future. As quickly as he had appeared, he disappeared again into the crowd like a worker bee before I could draw his attention. I then took up a more strategically obvious station but could not find him in the forest of taller people. I could not find him until he slipped his arm lovingly and assuredly around my waist and moved his head close to my ear and whispered, "Hello." I opted for the hug. Our music turned out to be the electronic-voice operated instructions digitally broadcast over the intercom.

The drive to the hotel and then to the restaurant was genuinely bizarre. Here in close proximity was an absolute stranger that I had claimed like luggage after an international flight from the airport. In our shyness, we were virtually utterly silent. My skills as a normally competent driver gave way to nervous wrong turns and lengthy explanations with exaggerated apologies. It wasn't until he began to speak that my brain put the virtual voice of the man I loved into the body of the stranger too close. Only then did I begin to relax and embark on the journey of getting to know the man who would eventually after many visits and nearly infinite long distance minutes say, "I will."

This is not where our story ends, but rather where it all began. Now each new day begins in my coveted silent aloneness before dawn, when the world and all my beloved still soundly slumber and when wee Moonie joins me quietly at the computer.

His eyes were open so wide, I thought that they would pop out of his head. He was kneeling on the floor, between the seats, rummaging through my tool box. Evidently, he didn't hear as I approached. I must have surprised him when I opened the door.

I was surprised too. I had left the cab of the telephone truck unlocked because I planned to eat my lunch there. I must have looked foolish, holding the door, my lunch and a cup of coffee. I tried not to drop everything when I jumped back.

The stress of the moment made him stammer, "I-I w-w-was looking for mmmatches..."

"Save it, "I interrupted." I know what you're doing. I have nothing worth stealing."

He reached for the handle of the passenger door.

"If you run I'll wave to those cops right behind me," I said.

He looked over my shoulder and saw the police car, at the curb, in front of the restaurant. He knew that he wouldn't get far before they grabbed him.

I'll stop myself, right here. For some reason, I can't just write a few declarative sentences when I have something to say. I have to tell a story.

To me, long stories with complex plots and many characters are an endless journey through the land of tedium. Perhaps, I have the attention span of a gnat. I don't know. Its hard work, but I prefer telling the story to getting to the point.

The incident I was writing about is true. I did catch a fifteen year old boy robbing my truck. His name was Jeffrey.

I had him clean up the mess he made and gave him one of my hamburgers. He kept glancing at the cops, sitting in their car, as he ate.

I asked him why he wasn't in school.

Jeffrey said, "They don't teach me nothin' there."

I handed him one of my stories and asked him to read it out loud. He read well. He didn't stumble over big words and seemed to understand the story.

When I asked him where he had learned to read, he just looked at me. So, I asked him how he liked my story.

"It sucks!" he said. He didn't like the way it ended.

"Why don't you write a story and you can end it the way that you like?" I asked.

Jeffrey fell into my little trap when he said, "I don't know how to write no story."

"Go back to school," I said, "and learn about double negatives while you're at it."

I gave Jeffrey an old book, an anthology of short stories. When I asked him if he needed a ride back to school, he declined. He said that he would ride his bike.

He thanked me as he got out of the truck. He unlocked his bicycle and put the lock in his pocket. He smiled at me and waved as he rode away, clutching the book I had given him.

This story tells you that I write because someone might get something out of it. I've already explained why I write short stories.

Two weeks later I was working in the same neighborhood.

I finished the job, put my tools away and got ready to go home. As I sat behind the wheel I noticed some things on the passenger seat.

Jeffrey had returned my book and a large screw driver.

I usually kept it in the box next to my seat. I hadn't noticed that it was missing. He also left a bicycle lock that he had used the tool to break.

A note, folded in the book, explained everything." Thanks for helping me. The lock was easy with that tool. I read the book. It SUX!"

I write fiction because a good lie always beats the boring old truth. Even if, "It SUX!"

Mourning Dove

"That woman makes me furious," I thought.

I was in the garage and had just repaired our lawn tractor. I was lying on the floor looking under the mower and trying to figure out where the extra bolt should go.

An inch away from my head, the door suddenly rose a few inches. It stopped and slammed back down to the floor.

My wife used the garage door button in the kitchen to call me. Since I had disabled the safety a few months ago, she wouldn't even be arrested if she decapitated me.

The door chopped at my head again.

"Mary knows how much that annoys me," I thought.

I couldn't see where the bolt should go. As I stood up, I thrust the bolt into my pants pocket and found another one there. It dawned on me that these bolts belonged in the toolbox in the pickup.

The door jumped again.

That woman makes me furious!" I thought.

My wife and I have been married for more than thirty years. I can say we've never had a fight; I can't say we've never argued.

The leak in the kitchen sink was ruining the cabinet. I shut off the water supply to the sink and told my wife I would fix it on the weekend.

Mary knows I am an expert procrastinator. Since she didn't want to wait at least a week for the kitchen sink, she called the plumber.

She also knows that the only thing I hate more than plumbing is paying someone to do it. I got very angry. I was down-right mad!

We seldom holler at each other. I displayed my anger by stomping out of the house and slamming the door.

I continued this petulant behavior by slamming the door of my old pickup when I got in. Then I kicked up a huge and satisfying cloud of dust when I roared down the unpaved road fronting our house.

When I was sure my wife wouldn't hear, I cursed out loud. The truck slipped, slid and bounced all over the dusty dirt road. The gardening tools I had in the back were flying around and clattering. I had to slow down.

After a while, I was reduced to mumbling and muttering as I cruised along at a sedate twenty-five miles per hour.

Suddenly, a small animal walked onto the road in front of me. I stomped on the brake pedal and threw up another cloud of dust as I skidded to a halt.

I was sure I had stopped in time, but I couldn't see anything. I got out of the pickup and looked underneath.

The animal that made me stop was a little, gray Mourning Dove. It was walking in small circles an inch or two short of instant death. The thing appeared to be confused. Maybe, it was in shock.

I spoke to the bird, "I didn't hit you, fella."

The dove stopped walking around and looked at me. He didn't totter out and flyaway.

"Come on. Get out of there," I said.

The bird didn't come out from under the truck. I bent over and waved my hand at the bird. It fluttered its wings but would not come out.

"Damn!" I muttered to myself and got down on my hands and knees.

"Git!" I shouted at the bird. It didn't move. I refused to be the instrument of its demise. Exasperated, I laid down on my stomach and crawled under the truck. I swatted the little bird out of there and sent it, rolling and fluttering, onto the road.

My shoulder touched the hot muffler, and I jumped reflexively and banged my head as I pulled myself out from under there.

"That was God getting me for smacking a little bird," I said to myself.

As I stood and brushed the dirt off, I saw the bird walk back under the truck. I leaned over and looked at him. He was standing in the same place, looking at me.

I knew he would not try to avoid me, so I crawled under the truck again and slapped my cap on top of him.

I carefully dragged him out of harm took him out of my cap and held him until I was ready to leave. Then, I tossed the dove off the road and drove away.

Looking in my rearview mirror, I saw the bird hop back onto the road. I drove for a few minutes and stopped.

My anger was spent but I was determined to cancel the appointment with the plumber. It was time to go home.

As I turned the pickup around, I muttered to myself, "That woman makes me furious."

The Mourning Dove was still there. He fluttered to the side of the road as I approached. It looked like he was going to let me go by. As I drove slowly past, we watched each other. As soon as I thought I might have passed by him safely, he charged under the truck. I stopped and opened the door.

Still seated in my truck, I swung my feet onto the road and bent my head down. I peered underneath. He was right there, waiting for me to finish him off.

As I looked at the stubborn little dove, I asked myself, "Why am I arguing with a suicidal pigeon?"

"Ok!" I said, "If that's the way you want it."

Something caught my eye as I turned to get behind the steering wheel. I got out of the truck and went to the side of the road for a closer look.

There was another Mourning Dove in the run-off ditch just off the road. She was lying on her back with her wings splayed. She had a broken neck.

"I didn't know you were mourning a loss," I said as I took the spade from the garden tools that were in my pickup.

"I'll take care of her," I said as I dug a hole next to the dead bird.

The other dove came out from under my truck and stood on the side of the road watching me, so I could not just shove his mate into the hole. I picked her up, folded her wings and smoothed her feathers. Then I placed her in her grave.

"Any last words?" I asked the mourning dove.

I looked around to make sure there were no human witnesses and pulled my ball-cap off.

"Saint Francis, watch over them," I said.

The dove continued to supervise from the side of the road

"For both of us, I'll say Amen," I said.

After I put my cap on, I used my hands to fill in the little grave. Then I tossed the spade into the back of the truck.

"Sorry for your loss," I. said to the bird as he stood on the side of the road and watched me leave.

Flying from tree to tree, the mourning dove followed me home. I hoped he wouldn't commit suicide when we got there.

My wife has a bird feeder hanging in a tree outside the kitchen window. She likes to watch the birds as she does the dishes.

When I got home, I saw the dove fly over to the feeder. I went there and pushed some seed onto the ground for him. Then I walked off a little way and watched to see if he would eat. The bird pecked at the fresh seed and sat down. He didn't seem interested.

Mary came out to see what I was doing. She stood next to me and looked at the mourning dove.

"Tom," she said, "I called the plumber and canceled the appointment."

Then she gestured at the bird and asked, "What's the matter with that Mourning Dove?"

I put my arm around her waist and said, "He misses his wife."

The dove picked up some seed and flew down the dirt road towards the little grave. In a few minutes, he returned and ate some more seed. Then he picked up some more and flew away again.

When we went in, I called the plumber.

Circles

Circles – eternal, infinite.
Intertwining Celtic knotwork
into the tapestry of our lives.

Spiraling through the warp and weft,
strongest where they meet.
Bound by invisible ties;
Friendship, Compassion, Love
Commitment and Trust.

Minds, hearts, souls
weave together into
circles.

Ever After

Once upon a time
the world was young
and so were we and
love and light and laughter
filled the hearts of
ladies and knights
and nights and days
and nights
spent on phone lines
destroyed by lines and lies
while he flies
and she cries
and trust dies
cannot resuscitate
or delineate boundaries

yesterday runs to
tomorrow
and the wind of change
blows through
and I threw
away your cards and letters
and I burned
for you
still
longing to drink my fill
of you
your smell and taste
gone to waste
waste not want not
don't let it all go to rot
and fill my dreams
and nightmares
of death
and lust consuming all
but love still burns hot
at the centre
of my being
still pure
but you're not there
any more
and all that's good
hangs from the rafter
and there is no
Happily Ever After

I Am She

I am She
> The Bearer of Wishes
>> and the weight of the world
My eyes hold the Knowledge of all things past
> and mysteries of times yet to come.
The Future but a twinkle and a wink
> or a wise nod.

I am She
> The Giver of Hope
>> or all of Pandora's troubles.
I hold out my hands with my gift to you
> shining bright for you to grasp
> if you dare.

I am She
> The Keeper of Secrets
>> that you whisper in silent prayers.
I know your Soul, your brightest wishes
> your darkest desires.

I am She
> Your White Virgin
Your Earth Mother
> nurturer and caregiver
Your Bloody Whore,
> eager to feast upon your offerings
>> and drain you of life.

I am She

Planning A Vacation On A Wet Winter Day

I'm slopping through the slush puddles,
Mucking in the mud.
I'm looking towards vacation time
Sure hope it's not a dud.

They said that it would snow today;
They said that it would stick.
But it is just too warm outside
This rain makes me say ick!

My sweetie came home late last night,
We played the whole night through.
He said lets go to New Zealand,
For nothing else will do.

I gave him hugs and kisses sweet.
The thought ran through my head,
"I love to just spend time with him,
even if its home in bed!"

Writing provides me with unique forms of both release and expression. I found myself unable to concentrate while I was the only programmer writing two wing structure design programs for a critical project at Boeing in 1966.

Journaling was a very effective way of off-loading the congestion of maintaining many details. In 1982, I learned to write poetry at the Jung Institute in Houston, Texas. After the deaths of my father and sister combined with a five-year span of sporadic unemployment, poetry deflected the full effects of these events.

Poetry gave me the chance to view these from outside myself and feel the balance I needed. The possibilities of this form opened a little more with each use.

The Placemat

The image on
    The placemat,
Is of a butterfly
    Approaching a rest spot
On a tall mushroom
    Offering a view.
There are herbs
    And roots,
Inviting leaves
    Everywhere.

This is quiet
    And of peace to us.

But in them
    It is
The business of life,
    Their fulfillment,
Crafted in millennia
    Uncounted.
They do it well
    In skill,
Beyond our measure
    Or cognition.

How long will
    It take us,
To learn from
    'waiting's wisdom',
To learn a hundred
    times more
Than we
    Now suppose?

Over this short time
    Of ego growth,
We have rushed to
    Claim understanding,
Spreading this like
    Thick jam
Over this
    Entire universe.

We feel profound
  Embarrassment
At the child's
  "Why questions".
They reveal the
  Transparently thin,
Nature of our
  Hallowed knowledge.

In our careful
  Reexamination,
Comes more stable
  Truth and diversity.
Deeper still is
  The realization
Of a more profound
  Nature, meaning, and life.

This life is how
  And where we live.
Embrace,
  Much as we can,
And we can realize
  The grander place,
Where we have lived, loved,
  And have tried to know.

BETTY YORK HARRIS

My inspiration for writing came from high school journalism. It opened a whole new world and way of expression for me. After marriage my writing was put on hold. Bill was in the military—a navy man. We were stationed in Iwakuni, Japan. The navy wives had nothing to do all day since our husbands were gone at least two weeks out of a month working at a factory supplying parts for airplanes.

About eighteen of us met at my house and I decided that we could start an independent newsletter about the who and what was going on around us. It also contained birth announcements, what was new at the PX and squadron news. This was a lot of fun for all of us and kept us busy. We named it the Anchor Echo. Since we had extra space in the paper the students on base had input. And it allowed projects for the girl scouts to help them get badges. The marines had a base paper and allowed us use of their facilities to print our paper. The Anchor Echo held us together and made us a family. Sometimes I wrote poems that started out as lyrics for songs, but only a few had music and this I have continued to do over the years.

Can There Be Peace

Peace is sought around the world
As danger lurks at every curve
I don't think it will come to be
Man will always disagree

We're such a diverse society
With pride and comfort for all to see
As far back as history goes
Man has fought soul for soul

Peace on earth, Good will toward men
Will these words be heard again
With each passing day war looms

Will this bring peace, or are we doomed

As in past wars, years, they may last
Innocent people always pay the price
Evil must be stopped I know
"Please" "Let Freedom Ring" from our lips flow

The Empty Old Chair

Everywhere I look it's there
The place you sat is now just bare
I never thought that I would care
I took for granted you in that chair
Memories follow me everywhere
No one to talk to and to share
I find myself standing at your empty chair
And now wondering where I go from here
I'll need some time to cry
Till God sits me by your side
Who would've thought an empty old chair
Would mean so much when you weren't there
MY-OH-MY what should I do next
Sell that old chair and fill its space
I'll find brand new things to take its place
So not a moment did I waste
You know I did and nothing changed
I still looked there and called your name
I never thought it meant so much
To have you sitting just across

A Little Glimpse From Heaven

This is as close to Heaven I'll get while alive
A chance to see earth from way up in the sky
Is it all I thought it would be?
Yes, oh yes, thanks to the wings

I looked below, how quite and serene
Mountains and rivers and small little streams
Cars looked like ants and houses with dreams
How picturesque, untarnished and clean

I saw puffy white clouds and beautiful blue sky
Plus two big silver wings, one on each side
I wished I could stay on this spiritual high
But no one knew better than that but I

I knew this plane would rapidly descend
And my beautiful dream would come to a end
There will be others along the way
Oh how I hope, oh how I pray

I will always remember this beautiful day!

The World Without Music

What if you turned the radio on
    There was no sound of music or song
    Just news & weather all day long
    Our souls lost like waves in a very dark storm

Could we dance, could we dream
    Without background music on which to lean
    Around the world music brings peace
    We share the rhythm, the words, the beat

Around the world each sound's unique
    From happy & sad & all in between.
    Music controls how we feel down inside
    It doesn't allow our emotions to hide

It has no limits but many goals
    It differs greatly from young to old
    It speaks its own language wherever we go
    Why can't we let music bring peace to our
    souls

As a child I was very shy. Eventually, I realized that I communicated better through the written word. My seventh grade teacher thought I was good at it and made me the editor of our newspaper. Writing brings me great joy and fulfillment. To see the look on people's faces when they read my stories and smile with a look of satisfaction is priceless.

Useless Harry

Shortly after the sun had set on top of the high school gymnasium, a new tenant was moving his furniture into Ida's boarding house.

Overseeing the event with partial indifference, Mrs. Idabelle the landlady leaned over her second-story back porch railing and glanced at the stranger through dark green eyes.

Blessed with the facial features of Elizabeth Taylor, she scratched her backside through an oversized pink terry cloth robe. Offsetting her fair skinned beauty, a body bulging with fat from too many meals of cornbread and pork chops threatened to come crashing through the creaking porch. She had attempted to lose some of her pounds by drinking a canned diet drink called "Sego." It was basically a meal in a can and contained about 150 calories per serving. Of course it didn't help much since she consumed about a case of the stuff a day.

"Miz Ida" as they called her, had two sons ages eleven and twelve. Her oldest "Sonny" inherited her wavy black hair and classic features but without the fat. Her youngest "Lonnie" looked like her late husband. He was a little chunky shaped boy with fair complexion and brown tangled hair.

As my brother and I were of the same respective ages and lived nearby, we were good friends of Ida's boys for half our lives.

Out of boyish curiosity, we all sat mesmerized on the fringes of the Kudzu vines, which attempted to overrun Ida's property, watching our new neighbor.

Glancing nervously over his shoulder at the four sets of eyes following his every move, the stranger shoved a chest of drawers and a coffee table through the door from the bed of a rusty pickup truck. Returning to the cab of the truck, he grabbed two mildewed covered suitcases and scurried into his basement room like a frightened fiddler crab.

Having sized him up sufficiently, we figured he was too old and ugly to get married and lived alone by choice.

"Harry Blum, that's his name. He's a switchman down at the railroad yard," Mrs. Ida yelled.

"Now get out of the Kudzu before a snake bites one of you."

Harry peeked out the window blinds through thick horn rimmed glasses, as we disappeared into the adjacent churchyard.

It soon became a common occurrence to see old Harry limping up the hill around Ida's house every morning at 7:30. He would pause briefly at the top of the driveway, adjust his glasses and resume his trek to the Southeastern Railway yard on Briarwood Avenue.

One humid morning we were sitting on the lawn at the top of the gravel driveway next to the boarding house. Lonnie saw old Harry trudging up the hill heading to work. Bored with summer vacation, he began chanting "Useless Harry, Useless Harry, got no friends, Useless Harry!" We all laughed and rolled around in the cool grass. Harry lowered his head, clenched his teeth, and hurried on down the sidewalk.

About a week later, my brother and I had just returned from a vacation to Oklahoma. We saw Sonny running down the hill from Ida's house. His eyes were filled with excitement. Between gulps of air he yelled, "Useless Harry killed himself! Useless Harry killed himself!"

We all sprinted up the hill and ogled intently through the open apartment door. A detective using a pencil gingerly lifted a piece of ragged shirt from the gaping chest wound. He then began explaining to his partner what Harry had done.

"You know it looks like he bought himself a new sixteen gauge shotgun. It still has the price tag on the trigger guard."

"Yeah, I guess the little mop stick was used to push the trigger when he set on the bed with the gun stock on the floor," his partner reckoned.

"Does he have any relatives we can notify?"

"No, the landlady says he was a widower and had no kids."

"Well, let's wrap this thing up. It looks like a good suicide to me."

Both men nodded their heads in agreement as the coroner drove down the driveway in a large black paneled truck.

After that exciting event, summer seemed to fly by quickly and since Sonny was a year older than me, he started high school in the fall. After that, he would have nothing to do with me since I was considered just a grammar school child. I hid my hurt feelings and found a new best friend the next year when I made it to high school. I never heard much about Sonny until about three years ago when his son called and asked if I'd come see him at South Fulton Hospital. He told me Sonny had terminal lung cancer and had only about three months to live.

Driving over to the hospital, memories of us playing football in the churchyard came to mind. We would steal some of my mother's flour from the kitchen and use it to line off a football field behind the church. We'd then play one on one tackle against each other and pretend like we were Georgia Tech football stars.

Walking down the hallway looking for room 304a, I was not quite sure what I'd find. Would he be a ninety-pound skeleton who could barely raise his head? I knocked on the door and his son answered. He was a tall boy with brown wavy hair and a lanky build. He looked like his mother who I hadn't seen in over 30 years. He smiled nervously and shook my hand.

"I'm Randy, come on in, Sonny is looking forward to seeing you."

I looked over his shoulder and saw Sonny sitting in a chair next to his bed in a hospital gown. Except for his black curly hair being cut short and looking a little overweight, he looked remarkably healthy.

"Hello, Sonny how goes it? I haven't seen you in twenty years!"

Sonny smiled weakly and replied "Yeah, we have our own lives to live."

"I hear you have two daughters."

"Yes, I'm very proud of them. One graduated from the University of Georgia last year and the other from Georgia Tech last week."

"I see you have a handsome intelligent son yourself."

Sonny smiled again and suddenly looked down at his hands.

"Hey Sonny, remember when we used to play cowboys down behind your mama's house? You were the Cisco Kid, and I was your sidekick, Pancho. I'd yell, 'Ohhhhhhhh, Cisco' and you'd yell back, 'Ohhhhhhhhh Pancho.' Then we'd laugh and laugh just like the TV stars."

"Oh, I don't remember any of that stuff anymore."

I thought he would remember our great times but I guess he had more important things to worry about now. I just walked over, bent down and gave Sonny a big hug.

"Well, Sonny goodbye."

He looked up and waved weakly. Randy smiled and hurried after me as I left the room.

"He was really glad to see you. I'm glad you came."

"Randy, you're a fine young man, and I'm really going to miss your Dad."

He smiled and turned around and went back into room 304a.

Driving back home I began thinking of Sonny's life since he'd left our old neighborhood. He'd gotten a job as a deputy sheriff and had two boys by his first wife Joann. Randy's brother had gotten hold of Sonny's service revolver and shot himself at the age of thirteen. His death so depressed his mother that she borrowed a pistol from a neighbor, rented out a motel room and shot herself as well.

As I drove up into my driveway, I heard the phone ringing in the house. I rushed inside and answered quickly.

"Who is it?"

"It's Lonnie, Sonny's brother."

"I know. I'd recognize your voice anywhere. I just got back from seeing your brother. I'm so sorry to hear about his cancer."

"Yeah, I cried and cried all last night."

"Well, how are you holding up? Is there anything I can do for you?"

"No, I just wish these neighborhood kids would leave me alone."

"They throw rocks on my porch every evening, and the other day, they put a dead turtle in my mailbox."

"I'm too old for this stuff. I live alone with my cat."

"You know, I believe they're going to be the death of me."

I suddenly heard a little boy's voice singing in my head.

"Useless Lonnie, Useless Lonnie, got no friends Useless Lonnie".

As my husband and I grew older, we would talk about "the good old days"; even though some of them weren't that "good" We talked about our childhood and early marriage. We thought our children would probably get some pleasure from reading about our lives, thus the beginning of my writing.

I jotted down notes on scraps of paper, backs of envelopes, and any other source of paper. I gathered records and really did a compilation of information, rather than individual thoughts. The book (which at that time was really just some stories) was started on the computer with an outline. As information was gathered, it was inserted into the appropriate place.

It appeared there were stories of relatives in WW II that I didn't previously know, so contacted the children or spouses to give me their facts.

Finally, it all came together and the decision was made to publish a book to share, not only with our children, but also with sisters, brothers, nieces, nephews, cousins, etc.

At the time, I didn't consider what I had done as "writing," however, it was well received by others and I was encouraged to write some more.

It is challenging, but appears something I enjoy. So I guess you could say, I "fell into writing"

The story for this book is based on fact. It seems I still don't have a talent for imaginary characters. Perhaps that can be developed with time.

Judged by God

It was a sultry, warm night in the 1970's. Not having central air-conditioning, the window unit hummed away in the bedroom to give a little relief. All of a sudden in the middle of the night, there was a banging on the front door. Who could be coming at that time of the night? Again, more banging, with a voice demanding to be let in. "Hey y'all, I'm here, come on and open the door."

Jim jumped out of bed, stopping to get two shells into the shotgun that stood by his dresser. Is it a burglar or a killer? The unloaded shotgun was kept behind the door for just such a situation.

Jim whispered to me, "Get up and go call the County Police." I awoke with a start. Did he say to call the police! I quietly went through the back den to reach the only phone in the house, which was in the kitchen.

Jim advanced into the living room to the solid wooden door. We had not put a "peep-hole" in the front door, as there was a storm door on the outside, which stayed locked. He opened the wooden door and in burst a man and pushed Jim back into the room. The storm door had not been locked.

Backing to get a good look at the man and assess the situation, Jim held the shotgun on him.

"Who are you, what do you want?" The man slurred some unintelligible words. "Get out or I'll shoot."

"Hey man, I must have the wrong house." The sight of a shotgun pointed directly at him must have sobered him up some.

I dialed the County Police number, no "911" number available at that time. Ring! Ring! "Hello, what can I help you with?" I quickly explained that we had a home invader and my husband was holding a shotgun on him. "Do you know the man? What is happening now? The police are on their way. Stay on the line until they get there."

As the man started to back up, Jim continued to talk with him. "Don't go anywhere." Finally the man backed to the door and opening the storm door, took off to his car which Jim could now see was pulled down to the brick wall. He had come across the yard and would have crashed into the house if the wall hadn't been there.

"I don't know who it is," I replied to the operator. "Please hurry."

"Just keep talking to me; the police will be there shortly. Are you in a safe place? Is there anyone else in the home?"

"Yes, I think so; our daughter is in the back bedroom sleeping. I didn't hear her wake."

KAPOW!

I froze with fear. Jim shot the man.

"Hello, ma'am, was that a gunshot?"

"Yes, I can't see what is happening."

"Stay on the line, the police are on the way." How long is it going to take, I thought. Is Jim all right? Come on, something needs to happen now. I heard the sirens; they will be here in a minute. "I hear the police."

"Stay on the line until a policeman can talk with me," she said.

We had moved into the neighborhood several years earlier. It was a dead-end street with several families.   It had seemed the perfect place to rear children. Recently, some of the homes had been sold or rented and the stability of the area had changed. The next-door neighbors had wild parties, lasting well into the night. Lots of drinking and loud noise and people coming and going.

The man didn't get into the car, but ran to the next house, where the door was opened for him.

The police came to the door, where Jim was standing, and asked what was going on.   Jim explained the man had forced his way into the house, had retreated to get into his car. Not wanting him to escape, Jim had shot the front tire of the car.

A policeman came into the house and talked to the operator on the line and told her everything was under control and that no one was hurt.

"Mr. Jones, do you know where the man went?"

"Yes sir, he went into the house next door."

"Do you want to press charges? We can't enter a house without a reason."

"Yes sir, I do," Jim answered.

They proceeded to go into the house, got the man, handcuffed him, and put him into the police car. "Mr. Jones, you will have to go to the Magistrate at the county and formally press charges."

After the phone call had ended, I went to see if our daughter was all right. She was still sleeping. I went into the living room and learned what had taken place. Thank goodness, the man wasn't shot.

Jim dressed and said he would be back in a little while. "O.K." I told him in a quivering voice. I went back to bed. Unable to fall asleep, I lay there thinking of all kinds of things that could have happened. I was still shaking.

Knock; knock, at the front door. What is it now? I got up and went to the now closed and locked door. "Ma'am, it is the police, we need to ask you some questions."

I spoke loudly through the door. "I will not open the door for anyone. You will have to wait until my husband returns."

Weeks passed before the summons announcing the trial date for the man arrived. Jim went to court where the judge, and the man and his attorney, appeared.

The judge began to speak, "Mr. Jones, I want you to know, I think you would have been within your rights to kill this man when he entered your home. That's what I would have done. He wouldn't be standing here today if it had been in my home. I have talked with him at length. He went out and got drunk and was going to the house next to you to get with a woman. His wife is expecting a baby. I want to know if you are willing to drop the charges based on this knowledge?"

Jim answered, "Yes sir, I will."

Speaking directly to the man, the judge spoke these words, "Young man, I expect you to get yourself into some help for your alcohol problem, and be a responsible man and take care of your family."

For a long time, I was very frightened at night. In the summer about a year later, a man came to the front door. The wooden door was open with only the screened storm-door between us.

"You don't remember me, but I want you to know, I'm the man who came into your home about a year ago. I have straightened up my life, have a son, an understanding wife, and we are doing fine. I want to thank Mr. Jones for changing my life."

I asked Jim why he made the decision he did. Jim said the man didn't really pose a threat and that he could see the man was drunk and obviously had come to the wrong house. However, he wanted to scare him by having him arrested. In those few moments, holding him in the sights of the gun, God had passed the judgment.

As far back as I can remember, I have had a passion for words. I always wrote – on paper, in dirt, on backs of magazines, on napkins, on lunch and grocery-store bags, and on just about any item that could serve as a holding place for my words. As the youngest of seven daughters, I often found that my thoughts were left unsung. I had a much better chance of being heard by putting words on paper instead of trying to speak above voices of older sisters. Of course, any sister would say that I spoke plenty! I was lucky being the baby and having the opportunity to observe all my sisters and participate in their activities, whenever I was allowed. My sisters provided an ample storehouse for multifarious ideas, characters, and stories; they all helped me to formulate my passion for words, and they taught me to look at the world and to appreciate the value of untarnished beauty in life's simple things. My sister Anne, whose hand I held for many years while I drifted into dreamland each night, told countless stories that she made up and then even quizzed me to assess my understanding. Anne's stories of a stooped, old woman in her flour-sack dress standing at a rickety gate crying into the night wind about long, lonesome nights made me want to hear more and more words from her. When Anne grew tired of my begging her for more stories, she simply said, "Now, Baby Teence, it is your turn. Let me hear your stories."

My true passion for writing poetry came when I started visiting an old family friend, Joe, in north Georgia. All my poetry evolves from times I have spent at Joe's homeplace and in his woods. I took trips there to relax and regain myself. While in Georgia's red-clay countryside, I spent most of the time either walking in the woods with Joe and his three Sheepdogs or waiting for sunrise or sunset on the back porch. Also, I spent treasured time with some local residents who have become more like family than friends. The people, the gospel singings in an old barn, the Christmas parades, the fresh, sweet corn from Valeria's garden, Zeke's Barbecue Stop with the yellow kittens asleep on the top concrete step, the rainy afternoon rides along the Blue Ridge Parkway, and the little white churches in the north Georgia countryside provided such beauty that I felt compelled to do more than simply enjoy the glorious moments and then leave there. I could not paint. I could not even draw. I knew, however, that I could not leave the beauty of the place untouched. I took out a journal, and I started to write. I write because I have to write, and I write because I choose to write. My hope is that in future days, my grandchildren's children will pick up some old, faded journals and know a little more about their Grandma's world.

A Taste of the Wild (Woman's Search)

A wild shrill calls us to places in night's wilderness
Where howls of wolves and cries of women meet.
We rove along damp earth and listen to the drum,
the whistle, the call,
And the cries from our true home.

We light a hidden lantern and begin our search.
Creak. Pull. Turn. As we cross bent twigs and wet pebbles,
We return an answer to the howling shadow who waits for us and
Encourages us to find the wild and instinctual nature
Far within.

We leap into the forest and run hard,
Our eyes scanning soft paths, our hearing sharply tuned, our arms reaching,
As we search for a remnant of light to reassert our relationship with
The wolf mentor, the force behind us, the guide before us
Whose voice beckons, "This way." Creak. Pull. Turn. "This way."

We move along deserts and oceans, cities and woods,

In barrios and in castles,
And we seek the mucky root of all women,
That ancient and vital wild woman, old beyond time.
We open the doors of our own lives and survey out-
of-the-way places.
We backtrack and loop and try to reestablish our
sovereignty
Over our own lives, and we cry, "Now it is our turn."
Howl...howl...howl.

We cavil in moonlight, tune our ears, make love, eat,
rest, and rove
In between. We write our secrets on the wall, and we
howl often as we
Struggle along matrilineal lines to reclaim a vast and
womanly wildness.

Daughters of daughters,
We travel from the wild and are born and reborn
From our dreams every day.
        And we sit by the fire and think about what
        song we will sing.

Enter the First
        wino that I saw sleeping on the street in New
        Orleans

where will you go when tomorrow's left-over-blues
        flow
        like fresh nursery curtains over your reeking raw
        fish soul lost in the day's collection of all you could
        drink
        two dollar and thirty-nine cents a pint
        sick sweet wine

that helped you find your bed
along this street called Canal?

...along this grey street you call home
that stops not at intersections but wanders
like barren garden paths toward the mighty river
on the other side of your open shelter's walls of
closed bars

where will you go when long lines of New Orleans'
rain
spill cherub tears onto your tattered newspaper
coverlet as St. Patrick's morning chimes
empty resonant chords of blessed assurances
into cheap cigar smoke-rings that linger
along this street called Canal?

...along this grey street that bids farewell
to late night blind lovers holding onto bitter vows
in back seats of yellow cabs that hum past
dawn's walkers who cover their half-filled coffee
cups as they step over
your broken pillow of rainbows
          and   say   nothing?

where will you go when you uncurl with quivering
moans and, inch by inch, stand to face
the backs of strangers who refused to look into
your eyes to see your battle with steel lids that
weigh upon you like chariots ruling the night with
iron whips"!

          Who   walks in sleep

                    ...along this street called Canal?

Forgotten Fruit Jars

four, fourteen, forty more
Fred kept bringing those
old glass jars from the shed
out back and lined
them up like fat trophies
across the side porch
lined them up tall
lined them up short
all standing proud
decorated with webs weaved long ago;
forgotten by everyone
but the night hawk who
flew close by and called
to his mate near the
fig tree heavy with unpicked fruit

......it's a cold river

it's a cold river
this run-down house
filled with leftover life
from yesterday's tenant
who spit on floors and
burned love letters in
a rusted iron skillet
on that little heater
near the window in
the front room
and watched Tom Allan's
words bum, burn away
like night's last stars
on a Wyoming prairie

Writing for me is both a functional and creative outlet. I write because I "have to", meaning that I professionally create many documents ranging from classified intelligence products to mundane processes and procedures for daily operations.

However, I also write because I "want to" write, which means finding enjoyment from the creative outlet and opportunity for expression, which only writing allows. I am not a "poet" by nature, but there are times, particularly after seeing or participating in events of great stress and magnitude, that can only be expressed in prose.

One Man's Journey

On March 19, 2003, the United States (with other help primarily from Great Britain) began combat operations against Saddam Hussein's Iraq. In the first part of my journey (published in Go With Us by the Fayette Writer's Guild) I briefly portrayed the stunning ground victory that was made possible by the professionalism, talents and sacrifices of the American Soldier. These successes were not without cost – for even victorious armies take casualties. Its one thing to talk in general terms about "acceptable" losses, it's quite another to actually see the casualties and the real aftermath of war. With the fall of Baghdad and the announcement by the President on May 1, 2003 that "major combat operations have ended" the war took on a new dimension. America's overwhelming advantages of military strength have been somewhat neutralized in the urban settings of Iraq. This situation allows a comparative few to fight on more equal terms the world's most powerful military. The "miracle" of 21 days of combat operations and the toppling of a corrupt and decaying regime has given way to months (and now years) of terrorist attacks, suicide (some would more correctly call them "homicide") bombers, and the realization that there was no "easy" victory. There are daily patrols, improvised explosive devices take a seemingly random toll, and it is sometimes difficult to understand one's place in the bigger picture.

Blossoming today,
Tomorrow shattered,
Life is like a delicate flower
Could one expect the fragrance to last forever?

Last equipment checks made,
Full ammo, water, campo gear,
But how to download and get rid of?
Your Spirit filled with fear.

People silently looking on,
Most stare with empty eyes,
As the patrol passes quickly by,
With a Spirit at least willing to try.

But it's also Soldiers filled with a strange pride,
Knowing so few know where they are,
Doing a job even fewer would do,
To protect families from afar.

Eyes on alert,
Constant strain and tension,
Moving through the hatred,
Spirit filled with dread.

Faces filled with hate,
Blank, hostile stares given back,
Its not anger which fills their hearts,
As much as love that they lack.

Troopers walking point,
Senses working at full speed,
Life and death lie in the balance,
Survival the overpowering need.

The lives of many,
Rest on the courage of so few,
Sacrifice upon sacrifice,
Battles nowhere near through.

Order,
Emerging from chaos everywhere.
Peace,
Bought at such a cost and price.
Hope,
Coming from a people filled with prayer.
Freedom,
Never free, coming from Soldiers lost.

When will the nation see....?   It's the Soldier who faces the greatest tests and threats. It's the Soldier on the ground, who, no matter what is said and written of technology becoming the master of the battlefield, will still have to face the enemy, suffer the deaths and wounds, face the agonies of losing friends and comrades, and face the separation from home and loved ones, in order to win. You can't look at their faces without feeling an unending pride and compassion for what they're suffering, how they stand firm in the face of adversity, and what they have and are accomplishing.

As night begins falling silently,
Soldiers gather close around,
Seeking out with active steps,
To search and clear this ground.

They seek a foe to vanquish,
Their defeat and death the goal,
And each step which they now take,
Proves it not a peaceful stroll.

Moving quietly with soberness,
They patrol and move about,
With strength, not boastful voice,
Neither with anger or with shouts.

To take life brings no one joy,
Its simply part of life,
For to bring peace to a violent land,
Must come through pain and strife.

The press is at best myopic, at worst biased and self-
serving. They claim to be "free", but are they? Their
judgments shape what they tell us and what we see.

They say they're fair and balanced,
With news and pictures clear,
But can we really truly trust them?
Do they a particular direction steer?

They claim always to be honest,
And bring us "facts" each day,
But we're finding that more and more,
They sacrifice truth for pay.

There are many Iraqis who like us – or at least want us there for a specific purpose and reason and see the good in what is taking place. Since Saddam fell, there have been untold advances. Hundreds of newspapers have sprung up, satellite dishes abound throughout the country, markets have blossomed, a stock market has been birthed, and while not all the news is rosy, it is far better on the ground than being broadcast on nightly news programs. I'm ambivalent about the Iraqi people – neither love nor hate. Children are different; it's always the children's faces where the future shines most bright.

Lifelines to the future,
Children growing old,
Learning to play and laugh,
At funny stories told.

Children skipping and laughing,
Freedoms never before known,
A heritage now purchased,
A future now owned.

But we should never forget that no matter how hard we try, we are still a conquering army and will be met with a conquered people's spirit – a spirit that can rise against us or treat us with a sort of benign acceptance. Whether the Iraqis are up to the tasks ahead remains to be seen, But it's their country and they have the most to gain – or to lose. We've sown into their victory and have seen that cost from the beginning. Is it worth it?

There is no time like the now,
But the time is forever lost,
We'll never know the true price paid,

We'll never know the cost.

Bittersweet memories,
Coming from hollow victories,
Casualties mounting,
Daily comes the Reaper,

The wounded and the maimed,
Crippled and bent,
Remind us pointedly,
Of the burden we have lent.

Lines of rifles upended,
Bayonets embedded in the sand,
Topped by helmets blood splattered,
Marking the cost paid for this land.

Caskets traveling home,
Three a day tolling,
No nearer the answer,
Quagmire now deeper.

The planes landing daily,
Disgorging tragic cargo,
Litters with wounded,
How could we know?

Ten a day wounded,
Ten a day more,
Ten more to the tally,
Ten more to the score.

It hasn't helped that "victory" was declared. On 1 July
2003 I recorded in "Growing Silence"

14 April 2003....
    We were told, guns would grow silent,
    The enemy would fold.

1 May 2003...
    It was spoken, from the deck of a mighty carrier,
    The enemy was broken.

1 July 2005...
    Nothing was said, while in the deafening silence,
    That we still bury our dead.

Their still faces,
Now forever silent,
Brought violently to an end,
Who will lament?

Will those who loved them?
Love them still?
Or will they soon forget?
Seemingly against their will?

Will the country that nurtured them?
Embrace them without delay?
Or will they be forgotten?
By the end of each televised day?

Throughout this process the one thing I am certain of is that I've truly grown to cordially hate civilians. They don't have to sacrifice anything, or suffer separation from their families, or face a violent death at any moment. I say "cordial" because part of me is glad that others don't have to face these hardships – that's one of the reasons we have a professional military. There is, however, something to be feared from this. If we ask sacrifices from only a few, then eventually, as in Vietnam, the nation will care little for the effort. Part of me wants to verbally lash out. I've always detested flag wavers anyway (those 4th of July patriots who never miss an occasion to raise the flag but somehow always have an excuse for why they couldn't serve in the military). The World War I poet, Siegfried Sasoon, on his first return from the trenches, wrote afterwards of a similar reaction,

You joyous crowds,
Who weep and cry,
And cheer when soldier lads march by,
Sneak home and pray you'll never know,
The Hell where youth and laughter go.

It was a bit disconcerting to be on the streets of Baghdad one morning and 24 hours later sitting in a sidewalk restaurant in Tampa and watching the "beautiful people" walk by. I'm told that returning military personnel are now given formal counseling and assistance to "readjust". I'm not sure if any amount of talk will help bridge the gap.

The Beautiful People
Walking by with no care
Will continue to exist
But not in foul weather, only fair

Worried about "things"
And so little more
They can't comprehend war
And the inherent gore

They know so little around them
Yet so much do they see
As long as its elsewhere

They're quick to agree

The beautiful people
So little they know
They won't face reality
Refusing to grow

The answer is of course
As their world collapses around them
They'll wail and lament
Like bricks with no cement

They see only what they see
And know only what they know
But are completely dead inside
Because they refuse to grow,

From head to toe fashioned
With clothes and jewels
What they seek is acceptance
Pride is their fuel

That we should fight the good fight
Expend all that we can
As long as it others
Who enter the butcher's fan

But if the carnage comes here
And cuts like a blade
Will they fall apart crying?
Will they finally be afraid?

They'll point fingers and shout
And cry out with fear
But the world will pass by

Without a care or a tear.

Yet, in spite of everything, I remain sure in my conviction there is something special about this country. We're certainly far from perfect, we can be self-righteous and sometimes hypocritical, but we can also be generous and selfless. We give more generously of ourselves than any other country in the world.

America is a special place,
Where dreams really do come true,
A place of sanctuary and of peace,
Desired by many, but known by so few.

Where a people have walked on the moon,
And reached for the stars,
Where hopes and desires don't fade,
And still draws people from afar.

Part of this journey is a debt owed to the past. In 1942 my Father volunteered for military service and also chose a combat arm (artillery). As an 18 year old he served in the Pacific, saw active combat in both the Philippines and Okinawa as a field artillery forward observer and became part of what is now called the "Greatest Generation". I knew little of his experiences while growing up. They were buried deep inside and as with many of that generation he wouldn't speak of them. His service, his sacrifice, his willingness to do what he did, will never be known. But I will remember – I will choose to honor them – in whatever way I can – I will choose not to forget. I was struck coming home by the massive differences in our transport to and from war and how the society of 1944 and today are in some ways vastly different.

I traveled home in luxury,
A first class plane seat my chair,
Being served a lap of luxury,
With diversions and no cares.

Different times and different places,
Same dreams and same faces,
We owe our country a life,
Even more when called to strife.

Sixty years ago my Father,
Traveled to war so differently,
Packed like cattle in a troopship,
With little care or thought of bother.

There is so much to be thankful for,
So much to return,
So little to ask for,
So much to be given.

The journey continues. Over the last two years much
has happened. We daily face a determined adversary
who is capable of launching attacks and spreading
destruction – but not of offering any form of alternative
– except death and violence. This is no Vietnam,
there is no beloved national figure leading the
opposition, no alternative being offered that many can
flock to. But there is death, and a rising level of
frustration amongst the American people. Whether
we stay the course or cut and run before the mission
is accomplished still remains to be seen. The press
has made a great deal of show concerning the "anti-
war" demonstrators. Polling numbers are held up like
the Holy Grail, as if a snapshot in time would
substitute for true knowledge of a nation's feelings.
But I've also seen in airports throughout the country

spontaneous applause and standing ovations for Soldiers, yellow ribbons on automobiles and friendly greetings for those in uniform. Yet, while that certainly is better than returning Vietnam Veterans received they cost nothing to the overwhelming number of Americans. Enlistments for the Army are falling short of the goals needed and parents of potential recruits – naturally worried about their children - raise the biggest objections to service. But an interesting phenomenon is also occurring, Soldiers who have been in the fight, who have witnessed first-hand what militants do to innocents, who have seen their friends injured and killed, are reenlisting in record numbers. No amount of bonuses paid, no college fund programs offered and no special perks can cause that to happen in the numbers they are. It means that for those few (out of the millions eligible) who have actually sacrificed for others, there are reasons evident enough to continue the fight. For them we should, as a nation, be grateful.......and somehow understands the cost......

They will never grow old
There faces will be forever frozen
In a time of youth
When they thought themselves eternal

They will look at us with faces
Unlined and unfilled with life's cares
Neither will they suffer or enjoy
The events that chart our days

They will always be young
Free no more to experience
Growing old, holding hands,
Nor feeling the sun on their back

They will look to us as faces on a page
Filled with quiet pride
Not fully comprehending what lies ahead
While they stand eternally on guard.

My mind bellows! My brain is packed full to over running with what I can imaginatively create. My psyche begs to give expression beyond what I can speak aloud. My sense of self insists that I write.

When I link words into something no one else has ever written, then read it and find it to be very good to sometimes more than wonderful, the thrill that hits my inner being is like manna; it nourishes me. My applauding audiences then uphold me.

My writings, my fictional endeavors as well as many stories of my life, beg to be shared. I take great joy when I do this. Some have titled me a "show off." If I am one? Well, I whole-heartedly agree to plead guilty, for I am convinced that writing is a gift I must not waste, it is something that I must not keep for myself.

My prayer is that I will continue to delight both myself, my readers, and my listeners with the words my mind roars out onto the written page.

Yes! Dear God, please let me roar!

Maker of My Soul

Maker of my soul, the me that I am, I send up my thanks.
When you sent me forth to live out my destiny,
I was so small and helpless.
When I entered this kingdom,
I was forced and not the master of my fate.
To where? To whom? I had no choice.
But this is where I am.
The entry to this place, your earthly kingdom, was so many things.
The coldness was first,
Yet I was provided warmth in my Mother's arms.

The sound was painfully thunderous,
Until I heard my Father's gentle voice.
The light was blinding,
But then, in one quick glimpse,
I saw their loving faces.
There was joyful laughter at my wrinkled face
And my precious nakedness.
Then at my Mother's breast,
Warmed and well touched
I was placed to taste the first of her sweet milk.
There was the fragrance of Mother and her giving milk
And murmuring love words to hear.
My senses? You knew they would come alive,
All gifts from you!
Well swaddled and given all comforts,
I will now sleep a while.
When I awaken,
I will wonder anew of where and who I am.
Oh, yes! Already I am greedy! I will want more
Of what I have thus far been given,
To feel warmth in caring arms,
To hear gentle voices and exciting sounds,
To see love in many faces,
To take in my Mother's scent,
To suckle more of her sweet milk,
To drift in the peace of slumber.
Yes! This earthly kingdom, too, is good! You chose
well to whom I came.
Maker of my soul, the me that I am,
I send up my thanks.

"MURDER IN SANDY LAKES:
The Journal of the Stranger Man"

By Pokey LaRuh

This Journal's End

My house on Sandy Lake? There is something spiritually scrumptious about awakening each morning in one's dream home. I begin each day with the freedom to seize joy in my senses.

Relaxed and eager to face the coming hours, I open my eyes, smile and stretch, or playfully roll from side to side in my king-size bed to get my old body tuned up. I also send up prayers of thanksgiving that I have, indeed, once more awakened!

I rejoice. I am happy I am a woman, happy that this body of mine has given itself to sexual pleasure. Joyful that I gave birth to the precious children I suckled. Delighted that I have a multitude of grandchildren, nieces, and nephews to love. Thankful that I have Jake, Mildred, and Patsy--yes, even Patsy--in my life.

I arise to meet the day and, depending on the weather, slip on my choice of worn chenille robe or beribboned peignoir. An almost daily, barefoot walk comes next. Going from my outer bedroom door on the south of my little mansion, I patter through my latticed and screened-in porch onto the veranda that wraps around across the front on the east, and ends at the side door on the north. My bare feet are greeted by the cool dampness of dew, the cold of snow and ice, or the warmth of summer sun.

What do I see? Always and for all my forever, there is Sandy Lake. Differing from day to day, each morning it has what I call a lake mood. Looking easterly season by season, the lake is transformed from sun-sparkled mini waves, to flat-gray slate, to small white-capped peaks, to ice or snow. God is surely saying, "It is good!"

I breathe in deeply. Depending on the wind of the moment, the breezes slip or careen toward me to deliver their gifts of what I call essence of lake. Sun has its scent. Rain brings its fresh fragrance. Snow delivers its clean bouquet.

In order to experience the touch of air during my time on the veranda, I raise my cozy robe or floating wrap to expose my legs, or I remove it and stand in my gown even at the risk of a chill. If I dared, I would walk naked as I have on nights when there is no moon. I tip up my face. My skin invites these caresses of morning air with its dry warmth, cool mist, or icy sting.

I listen to the wake-up orchestra of early day. Lake sounds, muted because of my hearing impairment, subtly greet me. Depending on the time of year, there is its swishy lapping, combined perhaps with the hum and whine of boats in their erratic to's and fro's.

There is the chattering of neighbors, the good-morning barking of dogs, a car horn reminding a slow poke to get moving, the calls of water fowl and the chirpings of song birds. Sometimes, especially in the winter, there is just silence, peaceful silence.

Hunger and thirst remind me that food and drink wait to satisfy that sense, that there is a breakfast to savor. Hot tea of many choices...juice, cool and sweet...cereal, crisp from a box or warm and soothing from the microwave...crunchy toast with margarine and marmalade or cinnamon and sugar...and sometimes the treat of crisp bacon and fried eggs.

My morning senses accept no interruption. No chores I must tackle. No job to rush to. No guilt to fret with. No murderer to catch; he must now meet his fate. I simply allow this assault on my senses as the sun, whether I can see it or not when the sky is cloudy, makes its way up, up into the sky.

Yes! The mornings are mine to enjoy, and I know I am truly blessed here in my perfect home on Sandy Lake, in Sandy Lakes, Indiana.

I still have all my teeth and most of my hair. I take George Burns' advice and drink lots of water before I go to bed just so I'll have to get up in the morning. I can still put on my socks standing up, however, some days I will lean on the wall. I've got a yard full of dogs, a cat and a bird. I talk to all of them and, although I'm the only one who understands, I swear they all talk back. I have the most patient and forgiving wife a man could ever want and she loves me despite the fact I can be a real pain to be around.

I stopped drinking beer from aluminum cans somewhat late in life and now don't trust my memory. Writing is the release I need to sleep at night. When I realized money and status were poor excuses for living, I started paying more attention to life's smaller details. I've been broke ever since but enjoy writing and embellishing on the everyday humor and passion that so often goes unnoticed.

At times I have to come to grips with my Walter Mitty alter ego when I feel myself becoming one of the walking, talking, comic book characters loose on our streets. Other times I feel significantly small and humbled as in the short story, "Reverend Freeman J. Johnson".

"Demons" is a brief glimpse of what may be considered my dark side, subjects I can't bring myself to talk about. The balance of those stories will have to be published posthumously to avoid answering a lot of questions. Writing is the vent for my humor as well as anxieties.

"No peace I find 'till I release my mind."

The Demons Never Sleep

What demons rule my sleep?
Wake me in anguish and almost to weep.
Transgressions past, never to be forgotten,
Names, faces, and places all remembered too often.

The images of demons with grotesque faces, evil eyes and stained teeth are those of myth and Hollywood. In the real world, each individual has demons with shapes and characters of their own. Some are tangible, in the form of excess or addiction and may seem the temporary face of comfort or escape. Many more are confined within ourselves with no apparent means of escape, or possibly worse, release.

My demons plague me worst when I need to sleep. I postpone going to bed, hoping I'll be too exhausted to remain awake, but it doesn't work. The lights are off, the house still, with only the occasional groan of a seal or rafter still settling. That's what my grandparents told me the noises were. Their house was fifty, maybe sixty years old. Still settling?

My demons are anxieties, unanswered questions, doubts, and failures. They manifest themselves in my weakest moments. When I'm at my lowest, the demons are at their worst. They conspire so that no resolution can be reached. Conspire, yet compete for dominance. My eyes close and a kaleidoscope of images flash and the causes of the demons take shape. People, places, and incidents linger in front of me for fleeting seconds but never gone too far or for very long. One problem conflicts with another, so it seems necessary to set priorities. When priorities are established, another factor is conceived which changes priorities. There is no answer, much less a conclusion.

Discovery at Dusk

Today I took the road less traveled. The further I drove, the more the appearance of the road changed. The pavement ran out, the trees formed a canopy and the road narrowed.

Through the trees, as the sun dipped below the horizon, there was still enough light to drive without the headlights. The light at that time of the day has a delicate balance. There's still enough to see silhouettes in the shadows but at distances the images are deceiving. The perception of size and distance is distorted.

This time of year the trees haven't filled out with blooms or leaves and treasures of years past manifest themselves. In the midst of scrub brush and vines are the remnants of a chimney. It stands in contrast to the woods and vegetation and opens the door to the possibilities of other structures. Stopping my truck, I strained in the waning light to see evidence of other treasures of days gone by. A few oblong rocks standing on end indicate the support for an old house, reminiscent of my grandparents' house.

I've discovered a few very large oaks or aged cedars are often good indicators of an old home place and it proved to be right tonight. A truly magnificent tree with limbs as large as my waist extending an easy twenty-five to thirty feet. The area surrounding the tree is unusually barren of the wild hedge and honeysuckle and within a few feet of the road is a skeleton, apparently of a deer.

A "Prairie Home Companion" is on the radio and Garrison Keelor is singing "What'll I Do?", a mournful pleading melodic song that always causes me to wish I could remember all the words.

A short distance ahead three deer walk briskly across the road, mindful of my presence but apparently not alarmed.

The length of the road could not be more than two or three miles, yet it took me thirty minutes to drive. There was so much to see, to speculate, and to wonder.   Time, location, atmosphere, and music came together in perfect harmony.

Growing Up With a Hat

If I was to sift through my mother's collection of my childhood pictures, close inspection would show at least one consistency. If the season was winter, or at least cool, I was wearing a hat.

I can remember a picture of Doug and myself standing outside my grandmother's house with our b b guns wearing thick coats and caps with ear flaps. I had a specific drawer in my dresser to put my stocking cap when I took it off to avoid having to look for it the next time I went outside. Then, losing my cap created as large a crisis as if I had lost my wallet today.

To say Mother preached the pitfalls of not wearing a hat is a serious understatement. To the best of my memory the discussion, one sided as it was, consisted of a few brief statements: "Where's your hat? It's cold outside. Don't go out without your hat." Twenty years later Mother played out the exact same scenario to my son and twenty years after that, again to his four year old daughter, Madison.   Mother's lesson has never changed.

My wife and I spent five days in Philadelphia, the week before Christmas. The temperature highs were in the high thirties to low forties. The area natives wore mostly sweats, light jackets and occasionally a stocking or ball cap. Bald guys wore their bare pates displayed like a Venice Beach body builder wears his tank top. Mother never told me some people do not wear hats and do not get sick. I was beginning to wonder if I had grown up under the inevitable promise of sickness follows those without hats.

For five days in the City of Brotherly Love I attempted to blend in with the natives and left my thick ball cap and wool Elliot Ness hat in the car. I attempted to walk on the side of the streets where the sun was shining and the wind was blocked by the buildings. Every time I stopped walking I tried to hide from the wind in the recesses of storefront doors. I was beginning to feel I had broken the chains of hat dependency.

I had not slept two consecutive hours on the morning we began our drive back to Fayetteville. My eyes felt full of sand and as if they were going to pop out of my head. My nose refused to permit oxygen to my brain, my lips were cracked, my mouth was dry and my throat felt as if I had swallowed a scrubbing pad. For over a thousand miles of interstate my nose tortured my head with alternating stuffiness to relentless running. Five days later, I was finally on the mend.

Mother, my hat is in the pocket of my jacket. I have an extra ball cap in the truck. I won't question your health guidance again.

My Small Space

I like to ride with the windows down. The roar of the wind is almost deafening but at the same time calming.

After a short while the noise is like a blanket and a shield. It envelopes me to the extent I think I can feel it touching me all over, almost heavy in its weight. A shield in the sense I am alone in my thoughts without interruption.

My arm rests along the length of the window, the skin beginning to feel somewhat oily from the humidity. My hand occasionally rotates at the wrist, fingers together to attempt to direct the current of air toward my face.

The radio had been turned up to compensate for the wind noise to the point it's an irregular squawk with indecipherable sounds. Now it's turned off and quickly forgotten.

Country roads at night are best when there's no schedule to keep. Narrow two lane roads between fields and woods with occasional mysterious eyes glowing from the glare of the headlights. The pace has slowed, no need to hurry. Like a great meal, it should be savored slowly, aware of all the qualities that make it special.

The fragrances of nature can only be enjoyed with the window down. Magnolias, gardenias, and honeysuckle, sweet and distinctive. Then there's a sweet musty, but distinctive smell of a swamp. The fragrances are always sharper at night.

Our world is connected by cement and asphalt veins. Many people drive with the air-conditioning on, the radio blaring, doors locked and windows up, protected in their "space". I like to ride with the windows down.

Reverend Freeman J. Johnson

This ageless road had weathered time with few significant changes. A slow progression from a hillside footpath possibly used by the Creek Indians to a muddy wagon trail and now a roughly paved road barely wide enough for cars to pass. It follows the edges of rolling hills and takes advantage of the limited rich bottom land that lies beside the river. By natural design the road dictates a slow pace to view the rural countryside.

Ralph and Billy grew up together in this pastoral setting and are modern day sharecroppers planting anywhere the limited tillable ground is available. They plant the fields of their neighbors and divide the result of their labor with the owners of the land. We have a similar agreement whereby our fields are planted with cabbage, pumpkins and beans. They maintain our hayfields in return for the hay for their cows.

Ralph had told me of a field of peas they had planted and told me to "pick a mess" for my wife. The field consisted of long rows parallel to the road and following the rolling contours of the hill. Beyond the field there was a small hilltop cemetery which appeared to have only a few graves and a couple of concrete angels. I turned onto a neatly trimmed drive and partway up the hill parked my truck next to the field of cabbage and peas. The cemetery was as neat as a putting green in contrast to the brownish color of the field.

My thoughts were just to a take a few moments to see the cemetery but the spectacle that unfolded demanded more. As I reached the top of the hill the panoramic view took my breath as abruptly as my first visit to the Grand Canyon. For possibly a mile or farther, gently rolling lush hayfields lined the opposite side of the Clinch River. Beyond the fields followed another higher ridge line parallel to the ridge where I was standing. Between the cemetery and the river the land rolled gently and pasture fences, now laced with honey suckle and dotted with small cedars crisscrossed the landscape. A solitary strand of wire separated the neat cemetery from the abandoned pasture. In one corner several apple trees struggled against the onslaught growth of weeds and vines.

To the east North Fork Ridge came to an end and as I looked at the peak the stark contrast of blue sky behind the lush green hardwoods contained one enormous tall pure white cloud. The green foliage, the azure sky and the white cloud held me spellbound for several minutes. It was good that I was alone because I couldn't speak. I could feel the knot in my throat growing. The end on my nose felt like pin pricks as the pressure under my eyes increased. How could anyone see all this and not be moved?

My attention turned to the cemetery and I first noticed all the headstones appeared to face the east. There were more stones than you could see from the road. Most bore the name Johnson with the earliest being Reverend Freeman J. Johnson, born in 1875. The stones told a sad story so common of the times. Birth and death dates being the same, some separated by a few days or a couple of months and many others by only a few years. Three sons and a daughter that never made it to their teens. Twins who died at birth.

The sun slipped behind the next ridge as I sat on the stacked stone wall between the two concrete angels. The only sounds were the field larks and a mockingbird in one of the apple trees. I thought about the eighty degree temperature, the tattered faded long sleeve shirt I was wearing but not aware of the heat.

This vision became a black and white image and I could imagine the person wearing overalls and a straw hat.

Reverend Johnson had lived through ninety-five years of the development of the automobile and airplane, Civil Wars and World Wars. He had weathered cold winters, summers with drought and the unpredictable flooding of the river. Despite all the hardships that were a way of life for the farmer, there can be no doubt the worst of it all was burying most his children on this hill within sight of his home. How often had he sat on this wall? Did the spectacle of the landscape touch him as it had me? Was it the inspiration that caused him to choose to become a preacher? Or was he humbled by the harsh life and heartbreak of death that he turned to God?

This Time Only A Spectator

Yesterday, I witnessed a Civil War reenactment. I was fortunate to be invited by my friend and enthusiast, Joe. He has a knack for telling a story and the ability to keep you hanging on each word in anticipation of the next line.

We walked the paths winding through Stately Oaks and looked at the displays in the encampment. Women in long sleeved, wool period dress, void of makeup, sweat beading on their brow while they tended large cast iron kettles and skillets over an open fire. I thought how dedicated to preserving the memory they had to be to sleep in tents and endure the eighty degree plus temperatures dressed as they were.

Men dressed in various uniforms cleaned weapons and smoked home made pipes. A few wore relatively new uniforms while those of others were faded with threadbare cuffs and collars bearing all the signs of wear and fatigue. An article I read several years ago regarding the making of the movie "Andersonville" came to mind. In hiring the extras, women, dressed as men, were used to portray prisoners because all of the men who applied were too well fed. This encampment was fortified with men who had not missed many meals. Again, the thought of the dedication of these men to portray the conditions over shadowed any thoughts of criticism.

Away from the encampment and near the antebellum home, tents were erected to sell period style uniforms and items to complement the attire. Among the tall trees in this less crude environment, more women strolled the grounds but dressed in the style of the well heeled Scarlet O'Hara we envision of that era. However, in an age of video games and internet, it was both strange and encouraging to see even young children take an interest in an event so far removed from their world.

Several hundred of us lined the outside of an elevated ridge to watch the battle begin. I decided there was a certain amount of choreography involved but I didn't understand what was happening because I wasn't aware of the events of the battle. A few of the Union soldiers rushed forward and crouched behind some fallen logs, more hid within the camouflage of the woods and brush while the majority hid behind the split rail fence and waited. In the distance and out of sight, the sound of a few shots could be heard and the Union soldiers became attentive and tense.

Far to our left, a few gray uniforms appeared, followed by more tattered uniforms who were closing into a tight formation. I could feel the tension, which was becoming all too familiar, as it etched their faces, many of which were mere boys. The sound of the drummer began softly and increased in volume though the formation had not moved. As they began to move forward deliberately and in unison, I was struck with the vision of the futility of their effort and the fatal results that would ensue. A Union cannon exploded and a knot in my throat started to swell. I couldn't help but notice as the combatants began firing at each other that it appeared only the grey uniforms were falling to the ground.

As the battle continued, I watched a young soldier's hat fly off as he suddenly arched his back and fell to the ground. I had to turn away as the tears welled up in my eyes. I took my bandana from my pocket and feigned wiping sweat from my brow as I dabbed the tears. I was thankful Joe wasn't watching or talking because I was beyond conversation and glad when it was over.

I'm not qualified to judge how realistic the battle may have been and that may only be a footnote to the experience. I would like to think the spectators were not expecting an award performance with professional actors and looked beyond the occasional lack of historical authenticity. The spectacle possibly hit a different nerve with me than the other observers. The waiting and anticipation, the tension and the first shot, and the sudden death took me to another war, a different time and place, different weapons and strategies, but with the same young faces falling to the ground. One hundred years between two wars with the same similarities recognized by this soldier. Whether it was fought in the woods of Stately Oaks or the dense vegetation of Vietnam, many in our country do not and will never realize the sacrifice required for freedom.   Many will condemn and thoughtlessly criticize war, yet do not realize all they have is because someone fought a war for all of us.

Who can I be today? How can I shape the world around me? Where do I want to go? What sights do I want to see as I travel?

Do I want to take anything or anyone with me as I travel or do I travel alone? Who will I meet along the way and how will they shape my world?

I ask myself these questions each day I devote to my writings. With my writings I am no longer myself with dishes to do, floors to sweep, and windows to wash. Forget that, I don't do windows and very seldom floors.

Imaginary playmates and invisible friends call to me, clamoring to let their voices be heard, asking for help through troubling times. Their destiny is in my hands. Are their lives happy and bright or full of sorrow and gloom? I get to decide.

Written expressions that feed the soul; tales of terror or times of glee, all are mine to decide. Short, snappy sonnets, fueling feuds, fjords to ford, and customized characters come from my fingertips.

The desire to create laughter for others to enjoy, emotions that are difficult to express face to face are fuel for my writings. Why do I write? I write because I must.

A thespian would say, "The show must go on".

An artist would say, "I must paint".

I say, "The story must be told".

Why do I write? I write because it is who I am.

Dealing with Doctors

Dealing with doctors is quite a chore,
> You give them all your notes and they want
> more,
> Gone are the days when the docs came to the
> house,
> Now I think many of them are a louse.
Oh, some are fine, and some are dandy.
> But when you need one none are handy.

You call the office and what do they say?
Sorry, but the doc is full today.
You have a growth, oh, that's just fine,
All you have to do is step up in line.
Looking over his notes, what shall it be?
Oh wait, the doc can see you in about week three.
You answer the ringing phone with glee,
But a recorded message is waiting for thee.
If you can see the doc on the time I say,
Press the pound key right away,
If you don't your name vanishes from view
And the time is given to the person on line two.
Dealing with the eye doctor and dentist is easier for us
They both have methods and schedules we can trust.
Your eyes go through changes each year or two.
The doc just mails you a note telling you what to do.
The dentist will keep your teeth neat and clean
All you have to do is visit his machine.
Our health changes, an undeniable fact,
But why can't the docs be on our track?
We give them money so we can be healthy.
And wind up helping the docs become wealthy.
Let's change the system and become a team
The docs should pay us when from good health we lean!

Fishing for your Birthday

Take a day of rest every year or two
    A day to relax, made just for you
    Swing in a hammock, enjoy a boat ride
    On the nearest lake, fishing poles at your side
If fishing is out of the question
    Here's something to look at while you're resting
    A boat at the dock, waiting in the calm
    Fishing pole in the ground just for your palm
A birthday should be a special treat
    This message I send for just you to read
    I know it's late, but only by a day
    You're my brother, none other do I have
Happy Birthday I cannot sing
    But good wishes I can surely bring
    So take the time and enjoy the view
    A painting created with thoughts of you.

Goodbye, Houston gridlock! Hello, alluring Asheville and the Blue Ridge Mountains! My husband's retirement prompted our moving adventure. We packed and headed "way out East" to North Carolina and later to Tennessee.

With children grown and out of the nest, my "kitchen duties" decreased considerably. How about a stimulating hobby to complete my recipe for retirement? Could writing be the answer?

I contacted National League of American Pen Women and found their Johnson City chapter filled with encouraging authors. By beginning with non-fiction, I could rely on many special memories for ingredients. My favorite stories mixed in bits of humor. Beyond encouragement, contacts with the writers and their stories of the area's history helped us feel very much at home.

However, the lure of an expected grandchild resulted in one more move. Our choice became Fayetteville for adoption as our latest "hometown." Having our first grandchild nearby proved a special treat.

After a time, I found and became a member of Fayette Writers Guild. The group has a wide variety of authors who act as literary "master chefs," aiding one another in presenting their toothsome "cuisine." Our Guild Hat Party provided inspiration for my first "partly-true" story.

I write in order to share memorable events, enjoyable trips, family history and to profile special people. Hope you enjoy!

Cousin Minnie Pearl

How-DEE! I'm just so proud to be here, just so glad I could come. Introducing myself this way always makes me think of my kinship with Minnie Pearl. Some folks even say I look a bit like her, with this hat and all. But, actually, I'm her cousin, Miss Prissy

Penworthy.   Minnie, rest her soul, has now gone to meet her maker.

Minnie Pearl was good to have as kin and generous as could be. Why, she even gave me this hat!   What you may not know is that Minnie wasn't one of us country folk at all.

In fact, her daddy, my uncle, was a big time lumber dealer in Centerville. I guess they named it Centerville because it's half way between the top and bottom of our grand state of Tennessee. She went from there to that uppity Ward Belmont College in Nashville and turned into an actress. She was good at dancing too and even taught others how to dance and act in places as far away as Atlanta.

Then our citified cousin got in with a bunch of stage people who toured all around putting on shows, singing and dancing for all who would come. But, it seemed like they would have a better turnout, if their act could get a little more "in tune" with the country folk.

So, Sarah Ophelia Colley became Minnie Pearl in a short skit to lure the "locals" to their show. Sarah got her idea from us country cousins in Grinder's Switch, and she always made mention of us. Everyone loved her, and when she got back to Centerville, they sent her straight to the Grand Ole Opry in Nashville.

Miss Minnie Pearl became a big star with all the fan mail and everything - even went on tour with Camel Caravan during World War II. It seemed like she just couldn't stop being busy.

She was everybody's friend for 56 years.

In Nashville, she married one of those airplane pilots and landed in all the best social circles as Sarah Cannon.   In the show, however, she never quite caught a husband. That didn't keep her from dishing out advice to the rest of us gals: "It may take face powder to catch a man, but it'll take baking powder to hold him!"

Excuse me, folks, I must run and mix up a batch of biscuits!

The author, Dorothy McLaren, is sometimes known as Miss Priscilla Penworthy.

The Quirky Trio

Oh, what a lovely wedding!   What a perfect couple! You're gaining another red-headed daughter! As parents of the groom, we took pleasure in all favorable comments. But, what about the blending? No one mentioned the extended family...

After all, the wedding of Scott and Mary was leading to a cottage, not just for two! Could Aloysius, Chester and Elizabeth find happiness in their new environment?

Aloysius, the beautiful, light-gray cockatiel, had been Mary's pet for a decade. His head was yellow with bright, rouge-like markings on his cheeks. Although named for a saint, his irreverent "wolf whistle" proved quite an attention getter.

Mary's second pet was Chester, the eight-year-old, very proud dachshund. His coat shone like a bright copper penny, and he fancied himself at least as big as a chow.   After first introduction, he maneuvered himself onto the sofa in order to gain some height and to survey his vast domain.

Chester had only managed to co-exist with Aloysius and always ignored the fluttery thing, even when the bird   was out of its cage.   Of course,

Chester grew lonely at times, but he could never be lonely enough to let Mary see him notice Aloysius.

Scott's faithful four-year-old companion was Elizabeth, the English pointer named for Britain's queen. She had to be introduced and have a bit of a "courtship" with Chester before Scott and Mary's wedding. At first, the sight of the long-legged beauty was a bit confusing to Chester. Elizabeth seemed shy and a bit frightened. Her willowy legs trembled with nervousness. He could not resist displaying his "big dog" image with a gruff bark or two.

However, after a few afternoons together, Chester and Elizabeth formed a warm friendship. Each had longed for a kindred soul when their master or mistress was away.

So, the two dogs were companions, but what about the lovely Aloysius? Who ever heard of a bird and a bird-dog sharing a home?

To our surprise, Elizabeth loved to watch Aloysius as he played in his cage. Fortunately, "Liz" seemed to instinctively know a cockatiel from a game bird. Her reward came with her discovery of bird food. Aloysius was a messy eater and constantly scattered food on the floor. Elizabeth had her snacks and "kept the platter clean."

The biggest household problem presented itself at mealtime with Chester. He only tolerated his diet food, prescribed when he began sagging too close to the floor. He much preferred Elizabeth's tempting fare and loved to watch for an opportunity to snatch a "Kibble" or a "Bit."

What about Aloysius, the lovely bird, perched high in his cage? When the situation became a bit chaotic, he did a fine job of whistlin' "Dixie!"

Time just flew when we had a chance to visit Scott, Mary and the "quirky trio."

But, those days are now past. The scene has changed. Each of the original trio has gone to glory. Plentiful pictures and a boat named "Miss Lizzie" make sure they are not forgotten.

In their place has come a new trio: three precious children, who run and play and create lively stories for a future day.

I started writing before I knew how to form letters. My parents tell me that I would sit down for long periods of time when I was three and four years old just writing squiggly lines on a blank page, and I would show them my writing with such pride. I think I was just fascinated by my ability to fill up a page with something I had done. I also was probably imitating my older brothers and parents. When I did learn to form letters and sentences I started writing short stories. My parents have kept my writings over the years, and on looking back at my thoughts when I was younger, I smile. It's just so funny what experience I've gained over the pen in comparison to when I had no knowledge of technicalities and mechanics of writing.

I started my first novel when I was in third grade. It was going to be a best-selling romance novel featuring Rosalyn and Clarence, the two lovers. What did I know about anything I was writing?

Nothing.

But the idea of people knowing me as the youngest best-selling author stuck in my mind through every syllable of my romance novel. I stopped on page forty-two when Clarence and Rosalyn were going to go upstairs. I didn't know what should happen after that, so I gave up.

I am an observer of the world and the people in it and I feel inspired by what I see and usually feel driven to capture it in print somehow. Writing stories and poems is my way to express the many things I feel inside, whether it is anger or revenge, happiness and joy, or even anxiety. So when something happens in my life or in life around me, writing is my way to capture it and make it my own.

Baby Language

She looks up and sees the trees
The Appalachian breeze,
Born of an ocean's tremor.
She takes in the smells, the warm
Delectable smells of beans and steak,
And Southern foods so foreign, so unrecognizable,
And she is secure in her peaceful thoughts—
Though none so far away can interpret them.

She is a child still so close
In the course of a new age: life 101.
The marvels and magic of nature
Bring about their beauty
Revealing their secrets only to her
Whilst the bodies moving around this child
Are wrapped up in their mortal
And finite fancies.
She doesn't understand,
But she will come to learn:
This is just the way it is, though changeable,
For many a day

As she looks up and observes
It in all its ultimate impregnability
She is trapped by it; she is spinning in bliss.
What more to do than coo.

Classic Break-up

I'm sorry; I just can't be with you anymore.
Trust me, this is not a mistake.
I know by doing this I'll lose a lot,
But it's for the better.

Man, I remember the days when
We used to really kick it—me on the couch and you
beside me.
If I neglected you for a day or two and came back to
you, there was no hardness about
You like some, as you were soft and welcoming.

Sometimes I'd throw you out, but I knew that you'd
always come back,
Even if I had to buy your affection...
It's always been sort of a sick relationship,
And that is one of the reasons we've got to stop this
terrible co-dependency.

It started when we were younger. You were my hero.
The bosses uprooted you, deep-fried you
And made your heart salty, and still you survived. You
survived.
But now it's time we went our separate ways.

Think of it as sort of a *let's just be friends, but nothing
serious* relationship.
Please understand, hold you in the utmost admiration.
You're just not the one.
Until the next *big hit, low-fat* potato chip comes
around, know that you were my first.

The Lesson

"I ain't nobody..."

Creator just absent-mindedly made me,
Braided me into strands of DNA that they call Me.

No one loves me, cause I'm different, cause
I don't got the hair, the face, the body of perfection.
But who does that leave?

You don't have to judge me, just overlook me.
I'll inevitably fall into a pit of love's opponent and
No one will know...

But you also don't have to be everyone else.
You could reach out, speak out, shout out
"THIS IS ENOUGH!" Be tuff Stand fo' justice
and pick me up.

What held you back? No one has got the slack
Pullin' and tuggin' till you can't do Jack.
Listen up, I'm right here, bellowing in your ear,
"I CAN BE SOMEBODY!"

In fact, I don't need that, the stressin' is just a lesson
Fo' me.
Thank you, Creator.
I can be somebody,
Scratch that; I am SOMEBODY.

When I was nine years-old, I sat down at my desk, which was two apple crates nailed together. My Mama had fancied it up by thumb-tacking a hogfeed sack to it.

With my pencil and Bluehorse notebook paper, I wrote a letter to my ex-lover. Eugene, who was once my darling, precious, sweetheart had written me a letter saying, "Sylvia, you are the ugliest girl in the school".

Eugene had gone from my darling to a devil. My sister, however, asked, "Sylvia, will you help me pick some daffodils?"

"No," I replied.

Picking daffodils would have to wait. I was on a mission. I had to write before I exploded! Three hours later my sister said, "Goodness, Sylvia has been writing for three hours without taking a break. She started writing long before Daddy went to work."

Mama answered, "Your Daddy had to leave home in time to stop at Austin's Service Station to get two dollars of gas in the Plymouth.

"Yeah", my brother said, "she is working as hard as Daddy, but Daddy gets paid every Thursday and can go to the Manufacturers National Bank."

Mama replied, "You never know what Thursdays will bring."

There were more Eugene's in my life, which meant I had to keep sharpening my pencil and buying more Bluehorse paper. While in the fifth grade, I became a published author. I didn't plan it. I was just doing my homework-writing a friendly letter. In my letter I used the names of television programs that were listed on channels 2, 5 and 11.

Not only did I get an A, but I was amazed that the entire class laughed at my finished assignment, even the teacher. I thought teachers never laughed at anything. In the same weekly paper that was published every Thursday—the town's only paper—where one could find the advertised specials, was my letter.

For the first time my Mama wasn't searching to find out where onions were on sale or if Kessler's had cinnamon colored hose for fifty-cents. She wanted to see my story and show it to everyone she knew. She proudly pointed it out to friends and family saying, "This was written by my daughter, the author."

Now, sitting at my desk, writing a monthly column for West Georgia Ladies magazine, I remember the apple box crate desk and Mama's words, "You never know what Thursdays will bring." Daddy and Mama have gone to Heaven. Kessler's Department store has closed, both Mr. Austin's have retired, and the Manufactures National Bank has changed its name. And me, I'm still writing—I'm on a mission. If I don't write I'll explode!

A Christmas Night To Remember

I shivered in the wet rain and raw, cold winter night wind as it whipped around the church freezing every bone in my body. I scurried   to get into the car before the weather turned my feet into Alaskan chunks of ice.

My husband, James,   quickly slipped under the steering wheel and started the ignition.   Waiting for the car to warm up and the windshield to defrost he said, "Whoo-wee, what a night!"   I didn't know if he was referring to the weather or the once in a life time performance he had just seen.

"Hurry and turn the heater on full power, super high or atomic blast or every what you do to get hot air blowing", I said rubbing my hands together trying to produce a small fire to defrost my fingers.

"I'm so tired I don't think my blood has run at all today.   I don't even think it got up!   And I'm starving - my stomach is caving in with hunger - I haven't had time to put a morsel of food in mouth all day!"

"I don't know if I am colder or hungrier-is hungrier a word?"   I ask pulling my purple wool cape closer around me.   "My front teeth are so cold they feel like a dangling icicle that's about to break lose .   If I don't get some hot coffee real soon to warm myself up and calm myself down I could be dangerous".

"Can't you drive a little bit faster-pretend like this is your race car. I won't complain one bit-I'll just hold on". After tonight's adventure I can do anything!"

The Huddle House windows were painted with beautiful Christmas murals and I paused to admire the holiday scenes of flowers, angels and candles. My nerves were not on edge-they had already jumped off-I didn't have the first nerve left. When my nerves jumped off they took my sweet-smelling magnolia scented deodorized underarms with them. I hoped the waitress didn't take one whiff of me and tell me to make myself comfortable in the back room with all the dirty, sour dishcloths and mops.

I was tired and aching from making props from thick pieces of cardboard for the past month. I had blisters on my hands and cut places on my fingers. My stomach felt like it was in knots, like all the horses had kicked me for accidentally cutting off their tails. Could I help it if I had to sew costumes in an overnight rush? Entering the front door, the mmm-mmm delicious smell of fresh perked coffee was so inviting it was almost romantic. It fact it said to me, "Hay, Miss Sibby I have been waiting for you".

The neon-lit juke box blasted out seasonal favorites as I collapsed my nerve-wrecked body into the nearest booth. Oh, the relaxing comfort of kicking off my black patent pumps and propping my size 9 narrow feet in my husband's lap. The petite waitress greeted us with Merry Christmas wishes and a menu. James ordered his usual unsweetened tea, hamburger steak and salad. Turning to me and adjusting her candy cane Christmas pen to write in red ink she ask, "What are you having?'

Trying to message all the pent-up tension from my neck and shoulders I replied. "A nervous breakdown!'

"I'll have 55 cups of regular coffee please and you can't get it to the table fast enough for me!"

I felt of my forehead to check my temperature. Bad as I felt I was certain it had gone up another 200 degrees. I was sure it was a case of stupidity fever from being talked into directing the church Christmas play-just one more time.

The shrilling sound of little girls bickering about which part they wanted still roared in my ears. Some wanted to be an angel with white feather wings wearing a shiny halo. Others wanted to play the part of a Bible character.   And I could still hear the heartfelt pleas of every girl. between the age of 4 to 16 asking if she could be "Mary".

Energetic two and three-year-olds were still whirling in my mind.   Images of them .dressed in animal costumes filling the stable where Jesus was born could definitely be a Norman Rockwell portrait.

Thinking about the months of preparation and final performance I knew it was truly a once in a life-time performance---

As the first graders begin to sing, "Away in a Manger", the toddlers listen tentatively for the words, "the cattle are lowing"-then they "lowed". Fifty rambunctious   children imitated sounds of cows, pigs, and   donkeys and other animals with their "neighing and 'braying, cooing and cackling. Next, they rolled in the hay, threw hay at one another, got up and "lowed" again.

The audience cackled themselves when I had to go to the stage   and whisper, "No,no, you are a "horsey"-you   can't get in the manger with Baby Jesus," which was followed by, "No, sweetie, you can't feed Baby Jesus a peanut butter sandwich right now".

The teenagers were eager to be a part of the program but they insisted I change the traditional manger scene. Half of the girls wanted to include a ferocious looking bulldog wearing a red sweater with a big "G" on the front and the others insisted a yellow jacket be perched high a big bale of hay. All the teen -age boys volunteered to play the part of the wise men and shepherds but the "wise men" insisted on carrying a sign that said, "Roll Tide". And the "shepherds" told me they could do a better job rounding up sheep with something that had wheels. I was tempted to tell the pastor that some of these creative actors and actresses had plans to replace the song, "Oh Little Town Of Bethlehem" with "When Stars Fell On Alabama," but I refrained because I saw no reason for both of us to have a heart attack.

I threw up my hands in desperation when they complained about the plaid flannel bathrobes the wise men would be wearing for costumes. I immediately knew what colors they wanted. Trying to convince me to let them have their way they said, "Now, Miss Sibby, this would be a good way to bring Jesus into the 'up-to-date new century scene".

I convinced them this would be a good way for "Miss Sibby" to be voted out of the church.. "Besides", I added, "Jesus is always up to date and he is on every scene before we even get there".

Program night had came and so did the parents, the grandparents, every Uncle and Aunt and everyone else they could pile into their car to enjoy this glorious time of the year. Everyone wanted to see their child, sing or speak or "low" or perform in an angel costume or be "Mary".

It was a moving experience. The children in the animal costumes managed to get out of the manger area and move to every area of the church. There was "mooing" in the aisles of the church and one little sheep "Ba,Ba,Ba,Baed" his way up on the highest hay loft and sung an entire song in sheep language. I managed to hear it above all the audience laughter and above another little "horsey" saying. "Well, hurry up and get through singing cause I gotta go to the bathroom". . And perhaps he did-because at that instant the stage curtain fell draping the cast in confusion. Looking for the children was like looking for Easter eggs under a deflated hot-air balloon.-a wet deflated hot-air balloon.

The shepherds were puzzled why their staffs had mysteriously disappeared and they were unhappy having to use the curtain rods from the Sunday school classes. They were certain the girls had something to do with this since the boys had refused to hike into the deep woods in 20 degree weather and haul back a 50 foot Christmas tree.

Someone cleverly slipped a big stuffed yellow jacket on the biggest hay bail-but the preacher immediately moved it to the toy bin in the nursery with the rest of the other stuffed animals. The look in his eyes as passed the teen-agers in the hallway told me somebody was going to be stung! Baby Jesus did start to cry halfway through the program, which surprised the toddlers and primary children .We had "moved' the porcelain doll and replaced it with a real live baby. Even with the baby crying you could hear one little voice standing in a cow costume saying, "Don't cry I'll give you my peanut butter sandwich ".

Slowly and carefully the second graders enter the stage carrying their battery operated hand held candles or at least they tried to enter that way. They were sidetracked when one little candle lighter stumbled, dropped her candle and the batteries hit the hardwood floor and rolled in every direction. She energetically chased them down by crawling under the entire middle section of church pews. It was at that instant the other candle lighters remembered what I had told them during rehearsals--"follow the lead candle lighter and do exactly what she does". Tonight, for the very first time-they followed my directions! The rest of the cast quickly banned the candles they were holding by placing them on bales of hay, or laying them on the floor or giving them to someone in the audience. They all began crawling on their hands and knees and bellies right behind her. They all crawled across everyone's feet, and each other.

You could hear them fussing at each other , "Move, get out of my way-your pushing on me-get off of my costume-help me I lost my halo-I'm suppose to be first-that's my Mama's feet - I don't see those batteries-where are they at."

Finally, the audience heard., "I gottcha you little aggravating rascals!" The pianist begin to softly play, "Silent Night Holy Night"', but all was not calm, all was not bright.

"Oh, 'Wittle' Town Of Bethlehem" will never be sung as sweet and neither will "Bo Tell It on the Mountain", even when a certain little angel gets her 2 front teeth.

Halo's fell off, costumes were tromped on, lines were forgotten, new words were added into songs, Mama's gave hugs, and children got candy. Little Drummer Boys drummed, and children sung songs about, 'A Christmas Night to Remember.' All. because one night a long time ago , "the little Lord Jesus lay down his sweet head".

Reminiscing about the final play production I said, "Lord, I am just thankful I didn't burn down the church," I said as I yawned. "Yes", I told my husband,

I can just imagine what the front page of the local newspaper would print: "Stupid youth director who was nominated the community idiot three times in a row, burns down church ". "Fifty-foot flames shot from a 20-bulb chandelier that she covered up with a sheet!

Yes, the church purchased the sheet! Didn't we tell you she was stupid!

Noticing a stinking odor that smelled like rotten eggs fermenting in a hen house in July, .the director said she dismissed the odor as:

1. A common body odor of all ladies directing church plays

2. The church deacons hiding in the broom closet to smoke.

3. The angel costumes that hadn't been washed in 20 years because the costume committee said it was sacrilegious.

I drank half my water taking a headache powders "My head is throbbing ", I told the waitress that was refilling the fake sugar holder. "I don't know if it's from my sinuses all stopped up from the fire or holding my breath for the last two hours afraid of what else could go wrong".

Slowly sipping on my black coffee I said, "Honey, I really am sorry about your hand". "If you hadn't seen that sheet and snatch it down and--- is it still burning bad?"

Taking my face gently between his hands and he brought his lips close to mine and in front of all the customers and staff he said, "BA, BA-BA--D"

Everyone had a instant remedy. The cook brought over baking soda saying that would take the burn out. The waitress gave him some antiseptic wipes and a customer offered aloe lotion she had in her purse. "I have a better idea I said, "Let me just stick my frozen feet on it - they need thawing out". That way both of us will have some relief".

The waitress looked at us and laughed as she refilled my coffee cup. I fished a piece of ice from my water glass and tried to convince him to hold it on the burned area.

He ordered a piece of chocolate pie and said, "Ah, honey, don't worry about it- what's a children's play director good for if she can't get all fired up!"

I wrote my first poem after my sister Elsie Williams of Thomaston, Georgia passed away. At that time, my writing was inspired by a deep sadness at the loss. As time passed by my inspiration came from the challenge and satisfaction of putting pen to paper and recalling life's experiences.
Now, I regard my writing as one of life's pleasures, bringing happiness to myself and hopefully enjoyment to someone, somewhere.

The Funeral Song
In memory of a friend, a bricklayer

A stillness echo's through the trees
And shimmers in the morning air,
I drink the quiet solitude
That manifests the silent prayer:
No whispered word or misted breath
Can still the loneliness of death.

Who'll tell the tale, who'll sing the hymn,
With teary eye recall the age;
With rhythmic tread play out the dirge,
Lamented by the sage.
The flame engulfs the fragile frame,
But not the given name.

He left it there on garden walls,
On dwellings in the vale,
In English bond and herringbone,
His work beyond the pale.
A void is cast, now he is gone,
An empty space, we'll miss you Non

The Lure

Bobby Braden watched his friend Tim Cook approach the house. He was carrying his fishing pole and a tackle box that was crammed full of lures, hooks, sinkers, and anything else he thought might give him an edge against fish he knew were smarter than people when it came down to survival.

While he was still about one hundred yards away he shouted. "Guess what I got for my birthday present?" and before Bobby could reply, "A new lure, guaranteed to catch a fish on every cast or your money back."

He arrived at the porch where Bobby was sitting and stood with his eyes bulging and out of breath.

Bobby looked at Tim for a moment, letting him calm down and then said "Tim, nobody can make a lure that's guaranteed to catch a fish on every cast. What if there aren't any fish around, how are you going to catch one?"

Tim plunged his hand into the tacklebox and pulled out a lure like a magician on stage pulling a rabbit from a hat. He held up a box that was about six inches long, cellophane on one side so the lure was visible.

"Just read what's on the box, look!" He then read aloud. "This lure will catch a fish on every cast guaranteed or your money back. If not completely satisfied return to manufacture for full refund. Made in China." The price of the lure was also on the box, one dollar.

Bobby smiled to himself and asked Tim. "If it doesn't work, how much do you think the postage will be to send it back to China?"

"I don't know," Tim said, looking a little deflated.

"Tim, when you get to be eleven years old you are supposed to have some smarts. Who gave you the lure for your birthday?"

Tim looked sad as it sank in. "My uncle Roger."

"And he's the one that's always playing tricks on you,right? Well he just played another one."

Tim sat in the chair next to Bobby and said nothing.

The boys lived five miles from town, both their houses sitting on the side of a mountain with a spectacular view of the Pacific Ocean. The lower slopes were thickly forested so they had the advantage of being able to play in the woods or to climb down the cliff path to the rocky beach where at times there were numerous pools of water trapped by the retreating tide, and several large caves in the cliff face.

Bobby it seemed had always taken charge. He was quite tall for his age and above average in strength and agility. He played soccer and baseball for his school and was captain of the sixth grade swim team. Bobby and Tim's parents worked, and had given up on baby-sitters two summers ago.

Mr Braden had bragged that Bobby could look after himself better in the woods or along the sea-shore than he could.

Neither boy had ever been in any serious trouble, just pranks, Bobby's father had confided to Tim's. "That's to be expected at their age."

"Well, we might as well try out the new lure Tim, if it only gets a fish on every other cast it will still be a bargain."

Bobby held on to the porch rail with both hands and howled with laughter. He slowly turned his head and could see Tim was getting annoyed, so he straightened up and said, "I'll get my gear and we'll go fishing."

The path going to the bottom of the cliff looked as if it had been carved out of the solid rock.

It was more than five feet wide most of the way and an easy climb up or down.

It ran south across the face of the cliff, and then about halfway, ran north to the beach. As the boys made there way down, the only noise they heard was the cry of a seagull and the quiet slap of the waves against the stony shore, the sea was flat calm and shimmered like glass, except for the swell it could have been a lake.

They carefully picked their way over the rocks and pools of water, keeping a sharp lookout for any large crabs or sizable fish.

Finally, they reached their favorite fishing spot, a large slab of rock with enough room to unload their gear and move around without tripping over it.

Bobby wasn't going to say anything about the lure. He had to turn his back on Tim a couple of times because every time he thought about the cast, the retrieve, and no fish, he wanted to burst out laughing, so without saying another word he cast his lure into the ocean. It zinged out a perfect cast, plopped into the water and was slowly retrieved, but not even a nibble. He watched as Tim attached his new lure and cast it out into the calm smooth water. It also made a loud plop as it hit the surface. He wound the handle of the reel fast, and then slow, fast and then slow again, trying in his mind to imitate a small fish feeding and playing in the plankton.

He had pulled the lure about halfway towards him when the rod was nearly yanked from his hands.

He had set the drag on the reel at five pounds and the line screamed as the fish headed for the deep. Tim had caught a lot offish in his young life, but could never remember a fish taking off like this. The rod was bent double and the line was peeling off fast.

The rod and reel were for sea fishing and Tim knew he had more than two thousand feet of line but the way this fish was running he was going to be out in a hurry. He thought of tightening the drag and risk loosing everything.

Then, as suddenly as it had begun it ended, the line went slack. Disappointed, Tim wound on the handle of the reel figuring he had lost the biggest fish he had ever hooked.

He could still feel something on the line, but no movement, so he thought he had probably hooked a piece of kelp. As he wound on the reel, he could see through the clear water it wasn't kelp but his lure, and it had swollen to three times its original size. As the lure hit the surface of the water there was a loud bang, and a flag shot out of the top which said "Happy Birthday."

Tim turned to look at Bobby, and there stood his Uncle Roger grinning from ear to ear.

He was holding a brand new fishing rod and a bag of assorted fishing gear.

"Here's your real birthday present Tim, I thought you might like this better."

Chickamauga

A shadow drifted through the trees
Black hooded, robed with crooked scythe,
And watched the battle scene unfold.
Brave drummer boy and ancient fife,
Clear musket shot and cannon roar
Sang out the melody of war.
The cheering throng charged to the fray.
The red blood fused with blue and gray.

The Chickamauga's water flowed...
Green woods and fields caressed her banks.
Two armies fate already sealed,
The marching thousands closed their ranks.
An early morning's whispered prayer
Each brave contestant well aware
Of horrors in the days ahead
Cool waters baptized with the dead.

The unforgiving leaden shot,
Tormented souls like driven hail,
Black swirling smoke, the thunderous roar
Of muskets echoed through the vale.
The fervent screams and sobbing breath,
For some the welcome hand of death.
Sweet thoughts of home, the uttered sigh,
Bemused, surprise, the last thoughts—why?

On Missionary Ridge they lay,
Blood soaked the soil on Snodgrass Hill.
Grim reaper drifted through the haze
And tallied names with sharpened quill
A note was made of circumstance,
Who perished mid the roaring guns?

Of Brothers killing ones they loved,
Of Fathers killing sons.

The Southern war of independence
Carried glories on the day
The battle cry was heard by all,
As gentle folk kneeled down to pray.
A prayer to end a savage war,
Unite a people, start anew,
For hands to reach out to each other
Past the folds of gray and blue.

Confederate soldiers stand with federals,
Spirits guarding sacred ground
At peace amid the stone memorials,
Whispering winds, the only sound.
Soft rains have cleaned the bloodied soil,
The hate which tore this land apart,
The healing hands of time will find
Forgiveness in the anguished heart.

Professional Mourning Service

If you are not affiliated with any club, church, or work related organization; are new in the neighborhood; have few friends; and are worried the attendance at your funeral will be less than adequate, we can solve your problem.

For seventy five dollars per mourner, we will mourn discreetly at your funeral, either soft sobs, or loud wailing:(your choice,) and for fifty dollars extra, or a minimum of six mourners, we will jump in the grave and throw the dirt out with our bare hands, while the grave diggers are trying to shovel it in.

Don't feel alone at the end.

Satisfaction guaranteed or your money back.

Rules For Charter Boat Captains, Crew, and Passengers.

1. The hymn *The Wise Man Builds His House upon a Rock* will not be sung or played on any of our vessels.
2. Do not anchor in a shipping lane or fairway, especially at night, sleep will not come easy. .
3. It is the captain's duty to apply the sun tan lotion to the ladies when they are sun bathing.
4. If taking excursions in town, it is not necessary to wear life jackets, people are not impressed.
5. Sea sickness will not be tolerated under any circumstances.
6. When the mate talks of rocket launchers, he is referring to rod holders in which to set your fishing poles not anti-terrorist paraphernalia.
7. Let the bait boy retrieve the hooks from the larger fishes' mouths, amputees are a hindrance to crew and passengers.
8. If it becomes necessary to rescue someone from the water, do not back over them. Pull them aboard with a line. Do not gaff them.
9. If the boat sinks, the captain and mate will have first choice in the two man life raft as they know the way back.

A Stormy Night in Georgia—A Play

Setting: A stormy night in Georgia

Location: A TV station news room and two storm-damaged outside locations.

Characters: TV station weatherman, (Freddie)
            Outside reporters,(Sloppy and Bernard)

Story: A severe weather reporting.

Freddie: Good evening. I have been hired as your weather reporter by this station ZIT because of my vast experience reporting the weather in England. I must admit I've been in a fog most of my life.
Right now we are tracking a dangerous storm moving across Georgia. Be aware this storm is packing a powerful punch. Expect heavy rain and some damaging hail. Tornado warnings are in effect for most of the metro area. Doppler radar indicates severe weather is shown at the location where our reporters are stationed. *This shot shows Dibley Road at the junction with Windjammer Lane.*
We will now go over to our man on the scene for a live report. Are you there, Sloppy?

Sloppy: Yes, I'm here Freddie. The situation here is quite desperate. A tornado was spotted in the parking lot of the Piggly Wiggly. It blew the wiper blades off of four cars, but left them undamaged. That's the way these storms are.   Earlier we had reports of wide spread power outages. Now, we are being advised that this was due to customers not paying their electricity bills and several expired light bulbs. Hold on. We have just been updated. Those wiper blades were the result of vandalism. I thought I felt a few drops of rain. The sky looks overcast and there were reports of thunder and lightning, which may or may not have been a car back firing. We will carry on our investigation into the bright flash of light. Back to you at the studio.

Freddie: Thank you Sloppy. The latest update on this strong line of storms is coming in as we speak. There is a strong suspicion the tornado spotted in the Piggly Wiggly parking lot has moved across the street, just missing the Wang King Chinese restaurant, and is now directly behind Wendy's. We will now go over to a new location three miles west. Are you there, Bernard? Can you hear me?

Bernard: Yes, I can hear you Freddie, loud and clear. I have just spoken to a gentleman that described the very same tornado that is now stationary in Wendy's parking lot. I asked him what it sounded like. He told me it sounded just like a tornado, definitely not like a freight train. It's still very dark. The devastation that I thought was the center of town has turned out to be the city dump; we are at the wrong location! Back to you at the studio Freddie.

Freddie: I am now on the phone with Mrs. Minnie---? Speak up please, this line is pretty bad—Glasshole, I thought that's what you said.

Explain what happened to you in the storm. Tell me what you experienced. *Short pause.* Nothing! You called to get the lotto numbers. *Back to our video at the Sloppy location.* Are you still there Sloppy.

Sloppy: Yes, Freddie, I'm still here. Daylight is approaching and we can now see the aftermath of this severe weather system. Although the pavement is almost dry , there does seem to be more leaves on the ground than usual. I seem to have the situation here under control, so I'll move on to Wendy's and check on the stationary tornado there and hopefully get some coffee. It's been a long night.

Freddie: A news flash has just come in. A chicken house in Gainesville has been completely distroyed. A veterinarian and counselors are on the way.
Stay tuned to this station on severe, or not so severe, weather in the future or days ahead. Remember, in the unlikely event that you are struck by lightning, move to the center of the house. Before we sign off, you will notice two telephone numbers on your screen. The station manager would like to conduct a poll with our audience, and the questions are 'Do you think the station manager is too good looking for his height, and our cameraman wants to know 'Is there anybody out there who would like a meaningful relationship with a happily married man?'
This will wind us up tonight, or vice versa. Have a great night.

Per Forming

The athlete knows the people are watching.
The people are usually back.
Behind a fence, in the stands, beyond the glass. There, but
not close.
A space between the athletic performer and the audience.

Usually, the athlete isn't alone.
He or she is with a team, as part of a larger ensemble,
or in competition with an opposite - a pitcher, a batter,
a defensive back, the other tennis player, the other
runners.

The musician, or the actor, knows the people are watching.
The people are usually right in the front row, and back row
after row.
The people are up close – personal like.
The musician, or actor, is performing with the other players
some of the time.
But often enough, they are out there all by themselves.
Solo.
Facing their audience.

Usually, this artistic performer can see past their audience,
put them out of focus, look away.
But often enough,
They look directly at their audience.

And perform –

My second year of graduate school in 2002, I became very ill and had to drop out. The pent-up emotions and feelings I've been battling these last few years inspired these poems. They reflect what I've endured mentally, physically, spiritually, and emotionally. Writing gives me peace of mind, peace of body and peace of soul.

Voices

I go to bed with voices in my head.
I thought it was the neighbors talking up stairs.
  Voices in my head.

They bother me all day.
They bother me all night.
  Voices in my head.

Some voices yelled obscenities
And some voices offering words of kindness.
  Voices in my head.

Slowly driving me insane.
I cannot sleep.
I forget to eat.
  Voices in my head.

When will the voices stop?!
Will relief ever come?
  Voices in my head.

Pills relieve the agony.
From the voices.

Voices in my head.

Familiar and unfamiliar
Call me by name.
Voices in my head.

Scare me to death.
Too consumed by the voices in my head.
Slowly I wither away, unaware.

With maternal concern, help was sought.
Finally, no more voices in my head.

Disappearances

One minute here, the next minute gone.
One minute seen, the next minute unseen.
Disappearances.

Families torn apart with broken hearts.
Wondering, praying day in and day out
When their loved ones will be found.
Disappearances.

Where could they be?
What could have happened to them?
Who could have seen them?
Disappearances.

Tips, clues, and possible sightings
Only lead to a dead end.
Days, months, years gone by still not a sign.
Disappearances.

Flyers fading, missing person files buried under
new cases of disappearances.

A Turning Point

This day is a turning point in my life.
Today I begin to live my life from the inside out.
I feel the transformation within me.
I am being transformed from the inside out.

God's spirit is within me.
When I come to a turning point in my life
I meet it with faith.
God is constantly preparing me for life.
Without God in my heart, the insecurities I feel
And the obstacles that stand in my way
Would be impossible for me to face.

As I prepare for this turning point in my life,
I accept God as my guiding light
To lead me through life's ups and downs.
So I let go and let God lead me on this,
The turning point of my life.

Feelings

Today, when I awoke I felt renewed.
It was as if my soul had received a new awakening.
I felt so light inside, as though I could fly.
I often wonder what this feeling is.

It makes you feel like a new person.
As if your body has received a new soul,

Or as though you had made another transition in life.
I feel that way often.
As if I have made yet another of many transitions in
life.

Sometimes my soul aches so bad, I feel as if I
want to die.
I wonder what that feeling is.
Is it your body rejecting the soul
Once it has used it for what it needed?
Or is your soul ready to reject the body because you
have yet another transition to make in life?

Mirage

One day I looked up towards the sky
And the heavens were revealed to me.
What I seen was a reflection of how this world use to
be
A long, long time ago.
There was lush valleys, flowing rivers,
Rich vegetation, grassy hills, and snow covered
mountains.
It looked so serene.
I believe I was the only one who could see this
awesome mirage.
It was so clear.
But slowly, it all disappeared.
Now this world is lost to me.
Still today, I look up towards the sky
Hoping and wishing to see this celestial mirage once
again.

Singing has and always will be my first passion. That's why I started writing. I wrote my first poem/song when I was thirteen. By the time I was fifteen, I had written twenty-one poems/songs. As far back as I can remember, my deepest desire has always been to someday be a famous singer/songwriter.

I didn't become the famous singer/songwriter I so wanted to be. I did, however, get the opportunity to do my thing as a singer, singing in local night clubs with a band that called themselves *The Watergate Band* out of Youngstown, Ohio in the early 1980's. Then again in Columbus, Ohio with an all female group in the late 1980's to the mid 1990's.

We called ourselves *A Touch Of Class*. They were fun gigs, and I had tons of fun.

In the late 1980's, I started working on a novel. My schedule was so hectic at the time that I had to shelf it. It wasn't until 9-11 that I decided to get serious about writing. I began to wonder about all the what-if's and all the unrealized dreams, so I decided to finish what I started.

During my writing sessions, I found that writing could be very relaxing. I'm in my own happy and peaceful little world when I'm writing. I write because it makes me happy. I write because it makes me feel fancy free and gives me peace of mind. Writing uplifts my mind, body and soul. Writing allows me the freedom to release my ocean of thoughts, dreams and fantasies.

Many of the opportunities offered to the young people today were not available when I was knee-high to a June-bug. It saddens me to the core when I see how so many of the young people today take for granted all the advantages they have at their fingertips.

Did You Pray Today?

Did you pray today,
my brothers and sisters?
Did you lift your head to the sky
to give God thanks and praise?

Did you lift your voice on high
and praise His holy name?

Did you pray today?
Did you take time out your busy day
to say, Father; Jehovah; Allah...,
I thank you for this blessed day?
Did you take time to thank Him
for the many blessings you have received?
And for the blessings yet to come?

Did you pray today?
Did you take time to send God a blessing,
as you went about your day?
Did you glorify His holy name
for guiding you safely through the day?

Say, did you remember Jesus
in your prayers, as you prayed today?
Did you send Him tons and tons
of thanks and praises for all
that He has done for you?

Hey there! Did you pray today?
It's never too late
you know, to glorify Him!
It only takes a second to look up...
and give God, the same respect
we give to doing our
favorite and fun things!

Tell me, my brothers and sisters,
did you pray today?
I prayed today.
I even took time to send
silent prayers your way.

And just to let you know,
each and everyone of you
are always in my prayers,
each and everyday.
Be blessed!

Prayers For The Mind, Body and Soul

Prayers For The Mind, Body and Soul is a collection of inspirational prayers. May every eye reading them and every ear that hears them receive through these prayers mental, physical, spiritual and emotional healing, as well as blessings and inspiration. I hope you enjoy reading them.

This is an awesome testimony that my friend Debra G. shared with me:
"The Lord longs to free us from whatever is holding us captive, and He has provided a way for us to accomplish this feat. Let us learn through the scripture how we may be set free. Consequently, he who is set free [by our Lord] is set free indeed!"

Now, please take a moment to unburden your mind. Relax and open your heart to focus on Christ Jesus. Allow the Heavenly father to be the only person on your mind as you read these prayers. Let the Almighty Lord God of all nations take possession of your heart, your life, and your time. Surrender yourself to Him that you may be set free mentally, physically and spiritually to be made worthy to receive Him.

WORDS FOR THOUGHT

Try to remember--not to forget, no matter how low or how high you get--Always look up! Have a blessed and safe day!

PRAYER

Heavenly Father, please know that even though the words of these prayers may be nothing more than meager, they are sincere. In the name of the Father, the Son and the Holy Spirit. Amen.

My Prayer For The People Throughout The World

I pray for the family and friends of all the loved ones who have gone on before us. I pray for the family and friends of all those who perished in the wake of 911, and in the wake of the terrorist attacks around the world and in London, July 2005. May their souls rest in peace! I pray for the family and friends of all the fallen heroes who gave their lives. May their souls rest in peace!

I pray for all the heroes still sacrificing themselves. I Pray that this War on Terrorism--and all the wars around the world--ends peacefully, soon and very soon! I pray for the family and friends of all those who perished due to Hurricane Katrina. May their souls rest in peace! I pray for those who are now displaced due to Hurricane Katrina and the storms that followed.

May they all receive the mental, physical, spiritual and emotional support they deserve and need. God bless all who lend a helping hand. This is my prayer for the world. Pray with me, in Jesus' holy name. Amen. In the name of the Father, the Son and the Holy Spirit. Amen.

Make Me Worthy

Lord, I know that no matter how hard I try, how good I am and how much I work to receive You, I am still a sinner not worthy of Your glory. Lord God, heavenly God, I know I will never, ever be worthy to receive You in this lifetime or in the next, unless You say the word to heal me mentally, physically and spiritually. I pray, in Jesus' glorious name. Amen. In the name of the Father, the Son and the Holy Spirit. Amen.

Guidance Through The Dark Times

Dear Heavenly Father, I am a believer who is struggling to keep faith alive. But I feel as if a dark cloud is hanging over my head and the world is closing in on me. I feel so overwhelmed and so burdened by my current [state your circumstance(s)] situation that I see only darkness in my future. Please give me the strength and the courage to follow Jesus faithfully through this dark time in my life. I ask that you help me to be patient and take things one day at a time.

I pray for strength, wisdom, courage and the peace of mind to accept things I know I can never change by not dwelling on the past. Please, dear God, I need Your help, Your love, Your guidance through this darkness. Lead me, guide me along the way. For only You can guide me through this darkness so that I cannot stray from the path that leads me to the right place at the right moment. My Lord, in the name of Jesus, I ask that You bless, give guidance and give strength to all the believers who are struggling to follow Him faithfully. Amen. In the name the Father, the Son and the Holy Spirit. Amen.

Strength, Courage And Wisdom

Dear Lord, I ask that You take rightful possession of my mind, body and soul. I beseech You, make me worthy to receive Your protection from any form of temptation I may encounter. I ask for the strength, the courage, the wisdom and the energy to maneuver around the rough terrain and over the steep hills that Satan has placed in my path. Please, help me derail Satan's defeat of me. In Jesus' name, I pray. Amen. In the name of the Father, the Son and the Holy Spirit. Amen.

Forgiveness

Most Gracious and Compassionate God, I implore Thee, forgive me this day for all my sins. Forgive me for all my thoughts, actions and spoken words that failed to please You. Please make me worthy to receive Your love, Your guidance, Your blessings and Your forgiveness. Dear God, soften my heart by Your mighty word and free my soul of any hate, anger or agony that I may begin to forgive.

For I know that in order to be forgiven, I must also forgive. I pray that we all repent and confess our sins to receive Your forgiveness, Lord. In Jesus' holy name, I pray. Amen. In the name of the Father, the Son and the Holy Spirit. Amen.

The Lost

Father of mercy, for non-believers who are lost and can't find the way, I ask that You enlighten them with open minds so they can accept all things. Please, I ask that You use me to do Your will. Let

Your love and grace emanate through me that when others are in my presence, their hearts will be touched by Your Holy Spirit. So much so, that Your love and grace will fill their hearts with an overwhelming urge to glorify You. I pray, in Jesus' glorious name. Amen. In the name of the Father, the Son and the Holy Spirit. Amen.

A Financial Blessing

Almighty and compassionate Father, I send up a prayer request with the faith that You will deliver me, everyone reading this or being read this, and each and every family member in our households, from debt encumbrances. And from any and all burdens causing mental, physical, spiritual and emotional stress. In the name of the Father, the Son and the Holy Spirit. I pray. Amen.

Guardian Angels

Most Loving Father, I ask that You send Your ministering spirits to guard me, guide me and keep me out of harms way as I go about my day to day life. From this day forth, may I live my life according to Your standards. May I no longer be swayed by insignificant things. And may Your ministering spirits give me reassuring evidence of Your never-ending love. To You I pray. In the name of the Father, the Son and the Holy Spirit. Amen.

Keep in mind, my sisters and brothers. "If God brings you to it, He will bring you through it."

To all my sisters and brothers: May God always bless you! May we always be grateful for those blessings! May God's messengers keep you out of harms way today and everyday! And may all your needs be met! Have a blessed and safe day!

'Twas The Night Of Halloween

'Twas the night of Halloween
And throughout every hood
All the creatures were stirrin'
Yes, even the mice...but its all good.

Glowing Jack-o-lanterns burned
In the windows with care.
While black cats prowled
With dark bristling hair.

The undead roamed
About in the hood
To gather souls
Be they bad or good.

The children were dressed
In costumes so sweet
Going door to door shouting,
"Trick or Treat!"

So you all better hustle
Hustle you hear!
You don't want to be caught
After dark out here!

Now, hurry dear children,
The witching hour is near!
The mischievous and grotesque

Ghouls are here!

    Scurry home dear children
To your snug, little beds.
The goblins are peeking
So cover your heads.

    If you tarry behind,
Or skip-a-beat,
This time next year
You can't trick or treat.

    Now sleep tight little children
The coast is clear.
Pleasant dreams and goodnight
See you next year.

Leap of Faith
Minowa WyldeFlower

"I am of age now," Young Chief announced to Mighty Warrior. "It is time you stop being my protector and just be my father."

Young Chief stepped outside his mud and straw built hut which sits upland. His right hand was extended palm down as he gestured towards the warriors posted near his hut and throughout the village.

"Let the men you trained to protect me and the prides earn their keep," he continued. "You have been a great guide and mighty protector. I will continue to look to you for guidance, father. But you must stop to smell the roses and fulfill your true destiny now."

"What are you talking about, my dear, glorious son? You have been my true destiny from the time you were born." Mighty Warrior professed as he joined Young Chief outside.

Motioning with both hands, Young Chief replied. "Look around you. Look behind you. While you were watching my back? Someone had your back, cleaning up your trail of errors.

The one of whom I speak is amongst a group of eligible young maidens the Elders have gathered from different prides for you to choose from. You must soon claim one as your mate. The Elders have informed me that from this day forth, she is your true destiny, your future, the future of all the Prides. You have no idea what you will be turning your back on if you reject her."

"I am a mighty warrior!" Mighty Warrior aggressively declared, striking his chest once with both fists. Annoyed, he stormed back inside.

"I have no time for a mate!" he exclaimed, continuing, "Though I find women of other prides to be rather beautiful, I have yet to find one that measures up to your mother or any of our women, for that matter."

"Yes! You are a mighty warrior and an equally proud man!" Young Chief implied, following Mighty Warrior back inside.

He paced back and forth as he resumed. "But that pride has clouded your mind, making you blind to your true destiny. Unless you let go of that arrogant attitude, you are going to be your own downfall, this pride's downfall. Besides, mother has been deceased for many years now, father. It is time you fulfill the prophecy by choosing one of the young maidens. If you defy the Elders or your chief, you will be banned

LEAP OF FAITH   171

from having sexual contact with any woman of this pride."

"My boy, why is it so important that I choose a mate from one of the other prides? What harm will it cause if I decide to choose a mate from our pride, instead?"

Young Chief took a seat beside Mighty Warrior on the bear fur covered log settee. He replied, "The prophecy foretells that a mighty warrior will unite with a young maiden from a distant Nativfrican pride. Their combined royalty bloodlines will produce generations of mighty warriors that will keep us dominant. By going against the prophecy and renouncing your destiny, you will be dooming our magic and mighty people to years of struggle."

Young Chief rose from the settee. . .all six-feet of him. He faced Mighty Warrior and placed his hands on Mighty Warrior's shoulders. "Now do you understand why it is so important that you follow the Elders advice and heed their warning?" he asked, his tone demanding.

Mighty Warrior breathe out heavily. "Yes. I suppose so," he responded. "But I'm not certain I am capable of choosing wisely. My choice in females has not been all that great since your mother. But. . .well, I'll give it my best shot."

"I have faith in you, father," Young Chief reassured Mighty Warrior, thumping him soundly on the shoulders. "From what I've been told, you have always made the right choices. If you observe closely, I am sure you will see that she possesses many of the same qualities that drew you to mother. It's up to you now to take a leap of faith."

Mighty Warrior was summonsed by the Elders. They gathered for the powwow at a hut in the mountainous section of the upland.

"Only one of the young maidens is your true destiny and she is highly fertile," the Elders informed Mighty Warrior.

"It is up to you to say the word when you are ready to meet them," they continued. "But there is very little time. You must marry and procreate with her within the month. You will only get one chance to make the right choice, so choose wisely, Mighty Warrior.

Stop! Look! Listen with your heart! And only with your heart!" They strongly advised. "Then and only then, will everything fall into place.

Do keep in mind, no woman of this Native African Pride shall ever be yours again. If you choose to ignore this, you will leave us with no choice but to exile you," the Elders firmly emphasized.

Two weeks into the month, Mighty Warrior was in dire need of the comfort of a woman. Concerned that he might succumb to his desires and stray off the chosen path, he confined himself to a cave high in the mountainous area. He ventured out to the upland in the late hours of night when he felt the coast was clear to bathe and swim in a nearby stream. Towards the middle of the third week, Mighty Warrior concluded that it was time he met and chose one of the young maidens.

Before returning to the village, Mighty Warrior decided to take his nightly swim in a secluded area behind a waterfall in the exotic gardens of the beautiful valley. Every colorful, scenery of the green valley is breathtaking with miles and miles of rich vegetation, roaming buffaloes, deer and wild stallions.

Mighty Warrior left his bareback pinto to graze in the fields of the upland and canoed down stream. He disrobed down to his buckskin loincloth after taking precautions to make sure he was alone. He secured his clothes and supplies high in a tree. He swam towards the waterfall after securing his spear and dagger firmly in a leather holster strapped across his shoulder. A warrior never ventures out without his weapon, especially at night. Upon entering the secluded area, Mighty Warrior heard what sounded like a woman weeping. The closer he got the clearer the weeping became.

There's no time to swim back for my clothes. She could be in danger or seriously injured. At least; I have the things that matters. My weapons, he silently thought.

Hoping she won't be frightened or offended by his appearance, Mighty Warrior hesitantly climbed onto the bank. To guard against assault, he readied his spear as he cautiously walked towards the light ahead. To his amazement, it was the light of the radiant moon reflecting off the aqua clear water. Brilliant stars lit the night sky, as well.

Mighty Warrior called out, "Hello! Is anybody there? Are you alright? Are you hurt?"

The weeping abruptly stopped. The next sound heard was the splashing of water. Frightened and nude, the young woman jumped into the water and hid. She was no where to be seen when Mighty Warrior made it to the spot the weeping derived from. After a careful inspection of his surroundings, he came across a weapon, a buckskin bikini type outfit with matching long armbands and a headband. Mighty Warrior briefly examined the items before calling out to her once more.

"Miss, are you okay?" He paused for a reply. "Are you hurt in any way?" Again he paused. "It's safe to come out. I mean you no harm. Please excuse my appearance, but it couldn't be helped. I promise to leave and let you get dressed once I see that you are okay. Miss, where are you?" he called out, yet again.

There was still no response from the woman, so Mighty Warrior walked to the edge of the bank to scour the water. At the exact moment he knelt down to take a closer look, she surfaced quickly, gasping for air. Caught by surprise, Mighty Warrior loss his balance and fell head first into the water. After regaining his composure, he noticed that she was standing in waist-deep water with her back towards him coughing uncontrollably. Mighty Warrior immediately rushed to aid her. He raised her arms above her head and delivered a few firm pats to her back. The young woman's coughing slowly subsided.

"Thank you, Mighty Warrior," Nubian Maiden said, offering him a soft smile when she turned to face him.

"You're very welcome," Mighty Warrior replied.

Although her curly locks of raven tresses which extends below her waist, shielded her voluptuous breast perfectly, that didn't prevent Nubian Maiden from placing her arms to her chest.

Mighty Warrior noticed that she was uncomfortable, so he stepped back a few feet putting distance between them.

Nubian Maiden studied him for a moment. His six-feet-plus brawny physique was irresistibly enticing as the water glistened on his cinnamon-brown skin. I see Mighty Warrior is still just as sinfully sexy as ever. And very well packaged, she mused.

She observed that he was just as nervous as she was. After envisioning his tumble into the water, she burst out laughing.

"I'm sorry--" Nubian Maiden was so overcome with laughter, she could barely speak. "I'm sorry for causing you to fall into the water earlier. But you should have seen the look on your face."

"You're just loving this, aren't you?" Mighty Warrior remarked. His ego a bit bruised.

Her laughter escalated upon seeing the chafe expression he displayed. "I'm sorry," Nubian Maiden managed to utter. She was laughing so hard she nearly lost her footing. She desperately gripped the rocks to maintain her balance.

Mighty Warrior fought back laughter and offered her a faint smiled instead. He made his way towards her and playfully splashed water in her face, sending some rushing into her mouth.

"It wasn't that funny," he commented.

Nubian Maiden gasped and spit the water out. "Alright, but you have to admit, I did startle you," she said with a giggle.

"Okay, you got me," Mighty Warrior reluctantly acknowledged. "Now I owe you one," he warned with a hearty chuckle as they splashed water back and forth.

She's as spirited and as beautiful as my late wife was. And just as sexy. Mmm. . .now if she was one of those young maidens, my decision wouldn't be difficult at all, Mighty Warrior contemplated.

"What brings you out so late, Mighty Warrior?"

"I couldn't sleep," he replied.

"Something I haven't been able to do for a while now," he added. "I have a huge decision to make in a few days, which could break or make me. So what's your story? Why were you in tears earlier?"

Nubian Maiden sighed softly as she turned her back to him. "My heart is heavy with sorrow because I have to leave yo— I-I mean, I have to leave those I love soon. I fear that I may never get to see any of them again, Mighty Warrior.

"Why do you hav—" He cut off as it dawned on him that that was the second time she called him by name.

"Not to change the subject, but how is it that you know me by name? Have we met before now?" Mighty Warrior inquired.

She turned to face him and proclaimed, "All the prides know of the Mighty defender.

Mighty Warrior cast a wide, dazzling smile in her direction. "Well you seem to have me at a disadvantage."

"Oh, pardon me for being so rude. I am Nubian Maiden of the Cheyene African Pride," she said, extending her hand with a soft, sensuous smile on her lips.

"Pleased to make your acquaintance, Nubian Maiden," he stated, flashing her a captivating grin.

Their eyes locked as he took her hand in his. The strong magnetic pull they felt made it almost difficult to tear their long, fixed stare away from the other's mentally seductive gaze. As Mighty Warrior gazed into Nubian Maiden's sensuous dark eyes, it no longer mattered that she was not of his pride. He saw her for the desirable Nubian beauty that she was. A beauty who was turning him on in ways that only his late wife had ever managed do until now. They glanced momentarily at the other's full, luscious lips.

Mmm. . .are those lips begging to be kiss as much as mine are, they both silently marveled with curiosity.

Nubian Maiden found the strength to break the hypnotic spell. She swallowed hard as she withdrew her hand from his gentle grip and took a few steps backwards. "I do believe you promised me some privacy so that I could get dress."

"I did, didn't I? And I always keep my promise. I'll go now that I know you're okay."

"You don't have to leave. Just turn around for a moment."

Nubian Maiden climbed out the water to dress as soon as Mighty Warrior turned away. Her lavender bikini outfit with fringed bottom and matching fringed armbands were highlighted with beading and raven feathers. Her headband was decorated with raven feathers and a beaded butterfly shape medallion.

Nubian Maiden continued the conversation while she dressed. "The answer to your last question is yes, we have met before now. And until a few months ago, I was in a way an unofficial warrior troop. And had been for many moons."

"I can't believe I don't remember ever meeting you," Mighty Warrior stated with a puzzled expression.

"You can turn around now," Nubian Maiden interjected.

"Tell—" Mighty Warrior was at a loss for words as he scanned her shapely physique. It was not until Nubian maiden sat down on the rocks with her feet in the water that he was able to gather his thoughts.

"Tell me, how did you come to be an unofficial warrior troop, per se?" he continued as he climbed out the water to sit beside her. "And how is it that I never knew of your existence within my troop until now? There are no women warriors within any troop, that I know of. Unless they are all posing as men. I-I can't see how such a beautiful and sexy woman like you could have possibly gone unnoticed by me."

"Thanks for the compliment. But the fact of the matter is, you rarely ever notice women outside your pride," Nubian Maiden remarked. "According to you, and I quote: 'No woman outside this pride is worthy my time!' You made that known loud and proudly too, I must add."

"I apologize for that insensitive remark, but I'm noticing now," Mighty Warrior commented in a low husky voice.

She smacked her lips and rolled her eyes. "Well, anyway, to finish answering your questions. I was trained to be what my pride call a Shadow Warrior. A Shadow Warrior is born every hundred years or so and is almost always female. Our purpose is to protect and keep watch over special warriors."

"Excuse me, Nubian Maiden," Mighty Warrior politely interjected, "but if you don't mind my asking, how exactly does a Shadow Warrior protect a warrior?! I wasn't aware that a warrior needed a protector."

"No, I don't mind the question at all. You see, our duty is to shadow that warrior and rectify the mistakes or unnecessary acts of that warrior by erasing all traces of damaging evidence. We never have personal contact with that warrior, unless special circumstances require it. We are responsible for that warrior until he retires or until his death or until we are needed elsewhere. And a few months ago the Elders informed me that my services were required elsewhere," Nubian Maiden stated as she gazed down at the water with a somber expression."

"Did they tell you where they were sending you?" Mighty Warrior asked.

She sighed softly and continued to stare down at the water. "The Elders told me I will know by the end of the month where that is. That's all they would tell me," she replied.

Distressed by the fact that she must leave soon, tears welled in her eyes. As the unshed tears were about to flow down her flawless reddish-brown face,

Nubian Maiden carefully slid back into the water not caring that she was dressed. She ducked her head under water to disguise the tears. Mighty Warrior observed the sadness in her eyes and sensed despair in her voice.

"Nubian Maiden, don't be discourage," he pleaded. "I'm absolutely certain anyone will be honored to have you in their presence. Myself included. It will be okay. You'll see," he tried to assure her. "It just might turn out to be an exciting adventure."

The comforting words of his sexy, deep voice and the charismatic smile he offered placed Nubian Maiden somewhat at ease. "Thank you for the compliment and the kind words, Mighty Warrior. But I really wish to stay where I am now. Especially near the one who holds my heart. Yet I know, I must go where I'm needed most." She could no longer fight back her tears and they begin to stream down her face.

The way the moonlight captured the beauty of her tear drenched face stirred Mighty Warrior's mental and physical being in ways no woman had ever come close to achieving. No longer able to resist the beckoning of her voluptuous lips, he joined Nubian Maiden in the water and drew her into his arms. His firm, moist mouth settled over hers. He kissed her with hungry desire. His male hardness pulsated with an achingly, sweet longing.

Her body throbbed with yearning as the rhythmic wrestling of their tongues mimicked their slow intimate dance. Mighty Warrior lifted Nubian Maiden onto the rocks and climbed out along side her. Their dripping wet bodies glistened in the moonlight. He gently laid her back caressing her body with tender kisses.

In the midst of undoing her top he paused and sat upright. "What am I thinking? I can't do this! I'm so sorry! Please forgive me! Please forgive me!"

"Mighty Warrior, calm down. It's okay. It's okay," Nubian Maiden responded, stroking his arm with a loving and gentle touch. After which, she readjusted her top.

"I can't allow myself to loose control! I almost blew it! We better get going while we still have the cover of darkness. The villagers will be stirring soon. Please forgive me for my selfish and impulsive behavior! I didn't mean to disrespect or offend you, Nubian Maiden!"

She took his face in her hands and stared into his eyes. "Calm down. It's okay. I don't feel disrespected or offended in the least. You weren't the only one to lose self control. Now stop apologizing. Okay?" she ordered.

Mighty Warrior took a deep breath. "Okay. I'm calm now." He took another deep breath. "I'm calm."

"Are you sure?" Nubian Maiden asked, offering him a sweet smile as she continued to gently cup his face in her hands.

The smile on her lips made it very difficult for Mighty Warrior to resist stilling another kiss. He swallowed hard, placed his hands over hers and offered her a broad grin instead. "You know, Nubian Maiden a beautiful woman such as yourself, should never be placed amongst wild, aggressive men. I hope the Elders won't be putting you in a similar situation like that again."

Nubian Maiden abruptly pulled her hands free. She glared daggers at him as she snorted under her breath. "Now I am offended! I can assure you that I can take care of myself! I can handle wild aggressive men as you call them! I've kept them in their place all this time!" she exclaimed, casting him a cold glare.

"I—I didn't mean to offend you. I don't doubt for one moment that you can take care of yourself. I just meant that— that—"

She let out a burst of laughter. "I don't believe it. Mighty Warrior is speechless. I have never seen you so nervous or speechless before. I'm sorry for snapping at you. I know you meant well. I'm just upset that the Elders are sending me away. I really love it here. I'm going to miss this beautiful valley and my favorite swimming spot. I'm especially going to miss you."

As Nubian Maiden sobbed, Mighty Warrior held her close. Gently stroking her hair, he whispered, "I'm going to miss you too, Nubian Maiden."

"I will never forget you," she said through tear drenched eyes.

"Nor I you. We will see each other again." Even if I have to defy the Elders, he mumbled.

The next afternoon, Mighty Warrior summonsed the young maidens to his hut one by one as Young Chief and the Elders looked on. He had his back turned each time one of the maidens entered the hut. Although he knew the Elders had other plans for Nubian Maiden, he silently hoped that when he turned around it would be her waiting to greet him. He was sorely disappointed each time.

Mighty Warrior intently studied each of the maidens before dismissing them. "Thanks for your time, ladies. You may go now." He directed his attention towards the Elders. "How many more?" he asked in a frustrated tone. "I have seen six maidens and none of them sparked my interest. I grow weary."

"There are five maidens remaining," the Elders replied. "You must take a mate before sunset tomorrow, whether or not your interest is sparked," they continued. "Now call in the next young maiden."

"Next," Mighty Warrior shouted with his back towards the door. He stood that way in silence for a full minute before acknowledging the young maiden.

"How long are you going to leave me standing here?"

Mighty Warrior instantly recognized the sweet, sexy voice that sang out. He promptly turned around and saw the gorgeous smile and beautiful features that had been engraved in his mind for the past twenty-four hours. He cast her a wide, dazzling smile. In two strides Mighty Warrior towered over her.

"Nubian Maiden? I-I thought you were long gone. How? Why? I don't understand."

"I learned a few hours ago that this was the new assignment."

"You're kidding."

"No. I kid you not, Mighty Warrior. This is my new assignment."

"Is this assignment acceptable to you, Nubian Maiden?"

"What do you mean? You know it's not up to me. I go where I'm needed."

"But if it was up to you, would you willingly take this assignment?"

"Yes. I would," she answered without hesitation. And what about you, Mighty Warrior. What do you want?" she added.

"Send the rest of the young maidens away," he ordered as he gazed into Nubian Maiden's eyes. He moved in closer. "I want you," he stated in no uncertain terms. Mighty Warrior drew her into his arms. His head dipped. As his mouth closed over hers, their lips parted, joining their hot tongues in a mating ritual.

Nubian Maiden slid her arms around his neck, pressing her body firmly against his.

"I believe we're finished here," the Elders announced, getting up from their seats.

"Great choice," Young Chief remarked.

They exit the hut one by one with a beaming smile of approval.

Mighty Warrior and Nubian Maiden were united as one two hours later. The waterfall where they first met became their own private getaway. They escaped there every chance they got. Nine months later, Nubian Maiden gave birth to a strong and healthy baby boy. Mighty Warrior fathered many offspring's.

Thus fulfilling the prophecy.

History Of A Native African Warrior Royalty Bloodline

Nubian Maiden has the soul of a spirit maiden. She is the great, great granddaughter of Butterfly Princess. The great-granddaughter of Native Queen. The granddaughter of Cheyenne Princess. The daughter of Mahogany Goddess and Cheyenne Spirit Warrior. . .the beginning of her Cheyenne-African bloodline.

Mighty Warrior has the soul of a tundra wolf. He is the great, great grandson of African King. The great grandson of African Warrior Prince. The grandson of Cherokee Chief and Nubian Princess. . .the beginning of his Cherokee African bloodline.

Mighty Warrior is the son of Warrior Chief and the father of Young Chief. He and Nubian Maiden parent many offspring's. Their mighty warrior offspring's: Whisper, Sky, Thunder, Night Hawk, Deer Hunter, Gray Wolf and Spirit Maiden all produced generations of mighty warriors.

The Native African Prides are a magic and mighty people. Now that the prophecy has been fulfilled, the legacy continues. . . .

Printed in the United States
40355LVS00004B/1-153